THIS AIN'T YOUR PATRIARCHS' POETRY BOOK;

CONNECTIONS, CANDLES, COMRADES....

Poetry fills the gaps and occupies the spaces between the study of sociology, law, politics, anthropology, history and literary analysis. Without poetry, cutting through the degrees of separation between schools of thought and filling in the blank spaces, which delete human emotions from the study of humanity, there can be no understanding of reality or the human condition. The authors of this book take the reader on a journey that cuts through all kinds of human separation and "cultural discontent"; it lays open "delegates of the wounded", faces all the "potholes"... "fears" and in the end "risks" squelching the desire for concatenation by refusing to shrink from any subject that alienates or fragments humans. In the end, it is the expression of difference that blurs the lines separating us from each other and overcomes that which alienates and fragments. The risks taken by the authors of this book create an heroic jaunt through the past, the present and point to a new future. I hope you all come to love the "skeletons" revistited, the "risks" taken, the "wounds delegated" and the subjects "gardened" by the authors who teach, inspire and transform the reader from inside the pages of this book.

Lee Maracle, scholar/Elder/professor at Western Washington University and author of Will's Garden; Bent Box, Ravensong, Bobbie Lee: Indian Rebel, I am Woman (and many other creative and/or autobiographical texts)

Patriarchal attitudes and discriminatory beliefs have caused a lot of trouble in this world. Social workers spend much of their time cleaning up the difficulties and discomforts caused by people who are stuck in rigid gender roles that only bring hardship to those around them. The writing in this book would be useful, and interesting, to many helping professionals as well as those people who seek their services.

Glen Schmidt, PhD; Chairperson, Social Work Program, University of Northern British Columbia

In a sometimes troubling and oppressive world, this unique collection written by eight women and four men, delivers a heartfelt, inspiring, and edgy tribute to the women who have powerfully influenced them in their own lives. The authors explore the despairs and strengths of women, with wit and passion. The timeless passages in this collection seem at first glance to defy all social convention, yet there remains a sense of tradition and the roots that bind us. This Ain't should be called This Is... As a social worker and a mother, this is required reading for social work students and practitioners alike, as well as the women, men, and children they know and love. This book is a testimony of hope reclaimed for generations to come.

Melanie Robitaille, MSW, RSW, Social Worker, IWK Health Centre for Women, Children, and Families, Halifax, Nova Scotia.

This is a powerful and touching collection of creative works – they are really impressive because they were written from the heart, they show women's and men's courage, and they are accessible to young and all alike. This collection is a treasure.
Marianne Gosztonyi Ainley, PhD. Past-President, Canadian Women's Studies Association, Professor Emeritus, Women's/Gender Studies and History, University of Northern British Columbia

The trick of life is to "see things in their separation and in their concatenation" [F. Engles]. When I first heard that I thought of Raven - our emotional and social transformer. I committed it to memory as the singular lesson I learned after 4 years of studying Sociological Theory. I let it
guide my life. Seeing things in their separation and concatenation is an emotional journey. At the time, the men in my class seemed to lack the guts to understand that life cannot be studied passively or analyzed dispassionately if understanding is what is sought. The men in the pages of
this book do not lack that courage...
Lee Maracle, scholar/Elder/professor at Western Washington University and author of Will's Garden; Bent Box, Ravensong, Bobbie Lee: Indian Rebel, I am Woman (and many other creative and/or autobiographical texts)

Looking for a provocative resource to stimulate critical conversation with Women's Studies students? This collection of poetry/ prose/ creative writing is a challenging counterpoint to more 'scholarly' resources. Lyrical while at the same time edgey, it is sure to get students thinking and talking about the complexities of gendered relations.
Diana L. Gustafson, PhD. Assistant Professor of Sociology, Brock University, St. Catherines, Ontario (& Editor of Care and Consequences)

In this volume, presented by a collective of eight women and four men, we hear the voices of people who feel with and for the women of the working world; with Wordsworth they hear "oftentimes the still sad music of humanity" and with Mikhail Sholokov they hold that books "should arouse ... a desire to fight actively for the ideal of humanity." They speak with deep passion about how: i have witnessed revolutions/& awed at how worlds can change over & over again/ within even one conversation... and look forward to a time when: Justice ? no longer blind/But with dancing laughing eyes, /bubbles beneath, between/ the ideas of women's worlds."
Uma Parameswaran, University of Winnipeg, in sisterhood.

The breadth of material in its variety and originality is fantastic. This anthology runs the gamut of ideas and imagery and is sure to satisfy the delights of any reader.
Janine Fuller, Manager of Little Sister's Bookstore in Vancouver

Enticing, that is the word that comes to my lips as I read the volume, "This Ain't Your Patriarchs' Poetry Book." It pulls you in, makes you want to read and know more, to go to the places of honour, vulnerability, love that the words create. This book crosses boundaries of genre, perspective, gender with the joy of a child jumping a creek. It is, of course, political but not ponderously so. It is about the pleasure and the challenge of living fully in a time that seeks fragmentation and dilution. The writers here refuse to buy into the fraying of human consciousness. Rather the poetry and prose in "This Ain't Your Patriarchs' Poetry Book" roots out connection with the past, with nature, with other women and with good men. If there is anything that ails you, anything that alienates you, this book is the antidote.

Dr. Mary-Ellen Kelm, Associate Professor, History; University of Northern British Columbia

This Ain't Your Patriarchs Poetry Book: Connections, Candles and Comrades is a text which is creative and memorable in the ways that it experiments with gender norms. The authors speak from First Nations perspectives, working-class perspectives, rural perspectives and these voices recognize that our commonalities and respect for our differences can sometimes unite and empower us.

Perry Shawana, LLB. Chair, First Nations Studies Program, University of Northern British Columbia

These "spirit-filled" authors come to this circle trailing their individual threads of color weaving together their experiences of patriarchy, oppression, and separation. Through their courageous words that bring forth their pain and hope,they remind us to birth other possibilities, and other realities yet unspoken. The smoking mirror of life reflects the vulnerabilities and dark places that humans hide and entrench their souls. These authors are fearless in their exploration of such unexamined secrets. Much like the shards of broken glass, this book gives you the opportunity to enter into the refracted spaces and explore the brilliance found in spirit spoken.
Teena Paul, Social Worker/ Policy Advisor, Aboriginal Affairs Secretariat. Government of New Brunswick(& mother, teacher, student, healer and friend...)

Like a shaft of sunlight shining into a darkened room, this book illuminates a pathway to new perceptions of women's realities. The authors, eight women and four men, speak with great sensitivity about women, and reveal the exquisite awareness of those valued men who know how to celebrate, appreciate, and honor women's strengths. This Ain't Your Patriarchs' Poetry Book engages the reader in an imaginative and grounded poetic conversation, informed by a feminism that celebrates the journey toward human well-being.
Jacqueline Baldwin, Author, Threadbare Like Lace, Caitlin Press, 1997.

THIS AIN'T YOUR PATRIARCHS' POETRY BOOK;

CONNECTIONS, CANDLES, COMRADES....

EDITED BY SI TRANSKEN

TRANSFORMATIVE COLLECTIVE PRESS

Transformative Collective Press
978 Central Street East,
Prince George, BC, V2M 3B8
sitran@telus.net

Cover Design and layout by PressForward
Typeset in Bookman Old Style
Printed and bound by PressForward

Transformative Collective Press
Paperback ISBN 0-9730571-1-4

We are the connections from the past to the future. We are the candles lighting darkness. We are comrades watching each other's backs. We ain't patriarchs or handmaidens to patriarchy's intentions. We are questioning and questing. We are opening our fine frontal lobes and fissured hearts and letting you peak inside. We are moments and mobilized in creative and continuing circles...

This Ain'ters, 2003

Two or three things I know for sure, and one is that I would rather go naked than wear the coat the world has made for me. Dorothy Allison. 1995. Two or Three Things I know for Sure. New York: Penguin Group. p. 71.

...facts don't always tell the truth, or a truth worth worrying about, and the truth in a good story - its resonance with our felt experience...sometimes must use imaginary facts. The emotional texture of experience often is what interests me - the consequences of the facts in the lives of actual persons. When I want to evoke the emotional texture of a human experience for an audience I find the canons of social science aren't very productive...I've been trained to make my academic research oriented to the factual, but my telling the story of that research is often disturbingly vacuous, because it lacks the traditional qualities of good storytelling, qualities like plot development...Character...My interest right now is to bring the two areas of questioning and doubt - factual reporting and fictional storytelling – into alignment, to see how my own streams of writing can be made to flow together... Anna Banks, 1998, 'The Struggle Over Facts and Fiction.' Fiction and Social Research: By Fire or Ice. Ed. Anna Banks and Stephen P. Banks. London: Altamira Press. pp. 11-12.

Given that cultural fascism is on the rise, that there is such open demand for separatist politics, embracing notions of inclusions and exclusion, whether based on shared gender, race, or nationality, seriously impedes all progressive effort to create a culture where border crossing enables both the sharing of resources and the production of a culture of communalism and mutuality. The fierce willingness to repudiate domination in a holistic manner is the starting point for progressive cultural revolution. bell hooks. 1994. Outlaw Culture: Resisting Representations. New York: Routledge. p. 6.

CONNECTIONS, CANDLES, COMRADES....

Inspirations come to us from a variety of locations and directions. The first two sections of this book present women talking about how other women (or girls, feminine spirit guides, 'mother' nature...) have supported and validated them. The third section of the book invites men to talk about the same themes. We share examples of how we have mentored and been mentored by feminist ideas and feminist practitioners/praxis (even if the words 'feminist' or 'women's liberation movements' were never spoken at the time). We have included our imaginative connections with women authors, artists, theorists - and strangers on the street. Some of our words are un/dressed in fiction; some in fact. Our voices have been in cooperative discussion for a year while preparing this book into the three sections we now share with you. Our voices could have been grouped differently and we invite our readers to regroup our writing as suits for their own life experiences and constellations of meanings. Please link our words and experiences to your own stories of connections, candles, and comrades.

The first section of this book demonstrates the complicated links and connections between and among women. We all have experienced moments of dis/empowerment. Some of us give vigorous thought to how we can resist oppressions and enhance each other's creative fortitude. We have been pondering how we have been developed by those around us. Jackie Hoekstra, Dani Pigeau, Ellen Winofsky and Maria Walther speak to (and with) women from the past/ present/ future who have taught about fortitude and spiritual strength. Jackie's background (as an English teacher in a variety of northern British Columbia contexts) enriches her poetry. Her roles as a mother and a spiritually grounded activist enhance her writing. Dani is a young First Nations single mother making

commentary on her experiences of racism - and her growing
strengths and confidence. Dani is a student (social work/
First Nations Studies/ creative writing), a community
member, and in the process of reclaiming some aspects of
her heritage. Her style of writing makes us remember that
the Official Queen's English isn't the only way of expressing
ourselves - and that the Queen *wasn't invited* to put her
words into the mouths of First Nations people. Ellen uses
imagery from Jungian therapy. Her experiences as a
traveler of the world; a mother; a social worker - all deepen
her compassionate gaze. Maria's background as an
immigrant/ scholar/ mother/ concerned citizen shape her
prose and poetry. Maria's poems most often speak to/about
female friendships and comradeships. It is possible also
that all of us, consciously or not, are communicating
something about motherhood/ mothering/ being mothered.

    In the second section of This Ain't... we explore more
of the links and connections between/ among the past/
present/ future. My section speaks about my experiences
growing up as a working-class person and an evolving
creative activist in Northern Ontario/ Toronto/ British
Columbia. Lynn Box movingly discusses her great
grandmother's contributions to the business community of
Northern British Columbia - and most significantly to the
well-being of her family. Theresa Healy articulates some of
the struggles of being differently mothered/ multi-
mothered; and of being an immigrant/ activist/ learner.
Yolanda Coppolino (a 71 year vibrant Italian immigrant
woman in Toronto) writes journal entries to Rachel Carson
(a 'spirit guide' who was an activist for environmental
issues). Yolanda's entries are focused on how she is
situated to care for - and become exhausted sometimes by
her caring for - her brave and strong mother (who is now
101 years old!). Yolanda could be defined as an elder,
talking to an elder, about an elder.

In the third section of this book we have welcomed men's voices. Clayton Boehler is a social worker in Vancouver. He has also been an activist in Northern British Columbia fighting for the rights of people who are fighting HIV/AIDs; who struggle with poverty; who resist homophobia. Rob Budde is an English Professor who also understands how vital it is to cultivate community through the arts. Will Morin is a professor in Northern Ontario; an artist; an activist on behalf of First Nations issues. Chuck Fraser is a union activist; an anti-poverty activist; a student; and a social worker. All of these men care deeply about the meaning of family in their lives. It is possible that all of us are communicating something about fatherhood/ fathering/ being fathered. These good men are activists who have been listening to, and living vigorously with, feminist ideas and intentions. These four men, like the other eight writers here, express some of the ways they learned to be like their parents - and/ or to strive to be the opposite of their parents in regards to gender expectations and 'performances'. These authors have been living those new ideas and intentions in their diverse personal/ political/ professional lives.

Connections, candles, and creativity are all around us. The poem presented below by Ken Belford was inspirational to me (the initiator of this publishing project) in many ways. This poem by Ken immediately invited me to remember interactions with my grandfather, Ken Purdy - who would never define himself as a feminist - in which he respected and admired my strengths. After his retirement (because of disability) from working in the mines, my grandfather and I spent many summers cutting wood, repairing docks, going for boat rides, gardening. As the first born grandchild and only daughter I was treated the way a boy might have been. Also, my grandmother's illnesses

(diabetic), and the fact that the three of us lived on an
island in the summer meant that my grandfather was
always preparing me to 'take care of things in case
something happened'. His attitudes and encouragements
evolved me into many of my feminist stances. The men in
this book are like Ken, like my grandfather, like many men[1]
- our comrades in trying to construct a different world.

   This poem from Ken Belford suggests his 'non-
patriarchal' values. He values his daughter's contributions
to the well-being of their isolated summer-time log cabin
home; he sees her as an autonomous creative person; he
doesn't appropriate her identity/ her labor/ her talents. His
gaze is peaceful. He communicates a high regard for her
autonomy and her connection with nature when he says,
"The waterhole and bridge/ were yours we thought, ours/

---

[1] In the pages of this book we explicitly and implicitly thank and
honor many people. Among the group of authors who wrote this
book there are hundreds of names we want to direct our political
and professional affections toward but here are a few that we felt
impelled to smile and bow to: Derek Wilkinson, Norman Denzin,
Karlton Terry, Bob Mullaly, Ken Collier, Victor Frankl, Henry
Morgantaler, Stuart Hall, Lenard Peltier, Barry Cotton, Ken
Calmain, Gary Kinsman, Gerald A.J. de Montigny, Irving
Goffman, Bruce Mulroy, Edward Soja, Michel Foucault, Cornel
West, Raymond Williams, Barry Wong, Martin Luther King,
Gandhi, Tommy Douglas, Cary Nelson, Gordon Ternawetsky,
Thomas King, Paolo Freire, Joseph Campbell, Lawrence
Grossberg, Ed Broadbent, Tom Wayman, Milton Acorn, Peter
Thompson, Neil Tudiver, Ross Klein, Robert Hoogendorn, Kwong
Tang, Glen Schmidt, Perry Shawana, Jacob Bolt... and the
millions of honorable men since the beginning of time who did try
harder/ take risks/ do the just and respectful thing for sisters,
daughters, mothers, comrades, unknown women, unknown
girls...

to cross and take from, to drink." Ken stands as witness to his daughter's natural beauty and the beauty of the natural environment around their home. This poem could be defined as an 'ecofeminist' poem. This poem could be thought of as a 'candle' lit to add more light to the space between a father and his daughter. We have gratefully reprinted **Runoff** in this book because it helped us, as writers, to focus on how men from different generations have also grown and enriched themselves with/ through/ in engagement of feminist ideas and practices. This poem could be read as an expression of the connections between one generation of supportive affectionate Beings and the next generation of 'nature protectors' or 'gentle responsible people'. Some men (and women) may have used different words to frame those feminist behaviors - and some of their behaviors could be read more than one way - but we have chosen to optimistically note and celebrate how some men (our comrades) have loved us into finding and being more of our strengths and talents. They have helped us find our magic.

Again, our intention is to invite the readers of this text into pondering how the men in their own lives have respectfully furthered women's goals; expanded women's safety and enriched our choices. Each of us has many identity pegs (gender, class, age, geographic location, ethnocultural affiliations, sexual orientation, religious beliefs, etc.). Gender webs into all the other identity pegs - and vice versa. Being able to understand and respond to our human complexity - with a mature comprehension of both differences/ distinctions AND commonalities/ connections brings more light into our individual worlds and into the larger wider world.

Runoff
> : for my daughter Hannah on the occasion of
> runoff at Blackwater in Spring of '99

Before you were the keeper
you were the maker
of the waterhole.
And I, pailing water this morning,
thought of things that seem to last.
We'd be there when the waters rose
each spring. The waterhole and bridge
were yours we thought, ours
to cross and take from, to drink.

Each spring you'd go
to the waterhole ready
with hoe and rake, rip
the retaining boulders out
and comb the deposited mud and sand away,
reorganizing the glut
that stopped the flow.

That last year you and I were together
before you left for the city
I regarded you with respect
as you mucked it out again,
setting the pipe and boulders just so.

That pool now gathers flow
year to year no matter what.
And that spring outside
our kitchen door still runs
cold and clear and pure and good.

The water flowed and filled our pail
those years our family lived

together under one roof,
a roof we made together, us three.

Do you remember the day
when just about to dip my pail,
we discovered the most lovely fish
we had ever seen?

Somehow through that trickle of water it came
over the boulders and into your pool.
The continuance: over and over now
that fish returns and
we who thought we knew so much
didn't know what it was.

Ken Belford, 2000, <u>Pathways into the Mountains</u>,
Prince George: Caitlin Press. pp 64-65

The acceptance and respect Ken gives voice to is the kind of unconditional love most women wish for from the men in their lives. This poem expresses a recognition too of the cycles of nature and how we are all embedded within those natural cycles - and with the creatures around us.

I have witnessed many women who have never had this experience (of 'unconditional love' from a member of their family - and especially never an unconditional strong love from a male member of their family). As a feminist therapist who has worked with issues such as incest, rape, wife assault, and depression I can attest to the pain some women have experienced in their dis/connection with men and patriarchal energy.

The writers of this book wanted to participate in providing material that celebrates men who have been inviting feminist assumptions into their lives. We wanted to celebrate men who are taking joy in the new ways of being. We wanted to celebrate women who celebrate women and feminist ways of seeing and being. As a professor in a social work program I teach courses such as 'Family and Couple Counseling', 'Social Work with Victims of Abuse' and 'Clinical Intervention Techniques'. Activists often make clear what it is that they don't want to happen - we wanted to speak about what we DO hope to find more of in the world. Our hope is that this book gives some examples of how we wish those who abuse or neglect women/ girls/ nature will change. Our hope is that young boys and men -- and the handmaidens who support them -- will be given these pages of text and that somehow our words will imprint upon their world views. Most importantly, we hope our words will change their relationships with all the females and female energies in their lives.

In Creative Optimistic Solidarity,
Si Transken, PhD, RSW
Assistant Professor, Social Work Program
University of Northern British Columbia

A LIST OF CONTENTS:

.....

A book begins as an idea. So does a social movement. So does a building. **We cast our dreams and desires ahead of us, and as we move toward them, their content takes on solidity. We cocreate our lives. This is both our responsibility and our privilege.** Julia Cameron. 2002. Walking in This World: The Practical Art of Creativity. New York: Putnam/ Penguin Books. p. 23.

Our culture has no niche for people who descend to the place of the big dream. Unless they happen to be artists, they have no place to take their gifts, and they risk being thought crazy if they speak of what they see. If they do not speak of it, they may in fact go crazy from carrying alone a burden of symbolic material that belongs to the culture as a whole, material that could heal our social wounds if we received and understood it. Janet O. Dallet, 1988, When the Spirits Come Back. Toronto: Inner City Books. p. 20.

'Allies' are distinguished by several characteristics: their sense of connection with other people, all other people; their grasp of the concept of collectivity and collective responsibility; their lack of an individualistic stance and ego, as opposed to a sense of self; their sense of process and change; their understanding of their own process of learning; their realistic sense of their own power – somewhere between all powerful and powerless; their grasp of 'power-with' as an alternative to 'power over;' their honest openness and lack of shame about their own limitations; their knowledge and sense of history [herstory]; their acceptance of struggle; their understanding that good intentions don't matter if there is no action against oppression; their knowledge of their own roots. These are the characteristics of allies; they are also the characteristics that mark people who are well advanced in their own liberation process. Anne Bishop, (1994) <u>Becoming an Ally: Breaking the Cycle of Oppression</u>. Halifax: Fernwood Publishing. p. 95,

THE WHO/ HOW/ WHERE
OF THIS CIRCLE OF CONVERSATION?

In this book we have come together as a circle of conversationalists who want to eclectically celebrate and acknowledge women's contributions to each other and to men's well-being. We want you to read these pages out loud - loudly! Our intention is that this book be bought as a gift for Mother's day; Father's day; International Women's Day; friendship days - any day when you want to thank someone who has mentored you with "feminine energy". We want you to ponder story telling and oral traditions. We want you to read these pages out gently.

The authors of this book have been active in a variety of struggles which have the goal of resisting/ stopping violence against women, children, nature. We share the value of non-imposition. We are parents, social workers, teachers, activists, students, researchers. We are immigrants/ visible minority/ settler/ working class/ middle class/ intellectuals/ pragmatists/ First Nations/ heterosexual/ gay/ lesbian/ bisexual... We were born into/ moved across/ are now in a variety of geographical locations – and our chronological locations are from early twenties to early seventies. We believe that patriarchy has linked with capitalism and hurt many many people in unspeakable ways. Oppression has become embedded in almost every dimension of our ordinary days as citizens of the world. In this book we have claimed this chance to speak our minds about our longing for a more fair and gentle world. As we bring this book to full fruition there are peace marches around the globe. The American war machine - with it's hypermacho stance - has just gone into a country far away from us in Canada. There is a temptation for Canadian citizens to have a lazy mind, a weak heart, and to disconnect from struggles so large and

far away. The writers of this book are at those marches for
peace; Take Back the Night marches; International
Women's Day marches. We organize and attend fundraisers
for women's causes. In our day-to-day practice and praxis
we attempt to make our visions for an equitable world come
true. This book itself will be used in a variety of ways as a
fundraiser for women's causes. We collectively and
individually pondered a list of questions (see below) for over
a year. We wanted to make vividly clear what our hopes
were for the different and positive future between the
genders/ ethnocultural groups/ vulnerable populations,
etc. We wanted to not only talk about **what we do NOT
want to have happen** around us but talk about **what we
DO want more of** in our lives. Our responses to these
questions constitute the book you are holding. Please hold
it with care and share it with those you care about - and
please, please also share this book with those people who
frighten you.

HOW WOULD WE, AS CREATIVE WRITERS AND SOCIAL ACTIVISTS RESPOND TO THE FOLLOWING PONDERINGS?

Was there ever a touching and particularly memorable moment that you experienced in a woman's circle/ a picket line/ a friendship circle/ your neighborhood/ with a female stranger?

What positive things or ambiguously encouraging things can you write about which show how women have lit candles in other women's lives?

What positive or ambiguously encouraging things can you talk about in regards to your comradeship with women's issues/ women's struggles?

What connections have you made / witnessed others make/ helped to make regarding women's solidarity?

What are you sure you have taught to women in your life? Can you describe a shared moment?

During your childhood, did a woman make a difference in your life? Can you describe a beautiful moment?

How could mentoring (directed at men and by men/ at boys by boys or men) about women/girls be enhanced?

Can you describe some moments in which you came to love yourself more deeply, wisely, imaginatively, powerfully (and in non-patriarchal ways/ non-oppressive ways) because of a woman's influence?

Who 'mothered' you well? Who coached you well?

Have you ever witnessed some splendid things a woman did for another woman?

Are there herstoric role models who have left magical footprints in the sand for you? Has there been an activist who taught you something special (even if that means that you learned by deciding to NOT do what she did)?

Who inspired your Muse? Given that the Muse is usually thought of as female; how come women/girls have such a hard time, sometimes, to just hang out with her and celebrate?

.....

Presently in America a war is being fought. Forget about guns, planes and bombs, the weapons from now on will be the newspapers, magazines, TV, shows, radio and FILM. The right has gotten BOLD... any piece of art that doesn't hold the party line is subject to attack. It's war in the battleground of culture. (Lee, 1992, p.xiii, also quoted by Watkins, 1998, p. 137) quoted in Norman Denzin's, Reading Race, p. 171. London: Sage Publications. 2002.

.....

The war is the first and only thing in the world today. The arts generally are not, nor is this writing a diversion from that for relief, a turning away. It is the war or part of it, merely a different sector of the field. Williams Carlos Williams, 1944. quoted in, The Collected Poems of William Carlos Williams, Vol. II, 1939-1962. p. 53. Ed. by Christopher MacGowan (1991) New York; New Directions Books

.....

1. CONNECTIONS
[THE LINKS BETWEEN / AMONG/ VOICES]

...cultural processes are intimately connected with social relations, especially with class relations and class formations, with sexual divisions, with the racial structuring of social relations and with age oppressions as a form of dependency... culture involves oppressions as a form of dependency... culture involves power and helps to produce asymmetries in the abilities of individuals and social groups to define and realize their needs... culture is neither an autonomous nor an externally determined field, but a site of social differences and struggles... Richard Johnson, 1996, 'What is Cultural Studies Anyway?', Ed. John Storey, What is Cultural Studies? New York: St. Mountain Press. p. 76

'Research' is just something we're doing every day every where we go when we're paying attention....

Feminists choose multiple methods for technical reasons, similar to mainstream researchers, and for particular feminist concerns that reflect intellectual, emotional, and political commitments. Feminist descriptions of multimethods research express the commitment to thoroughness, the desire to be open-ended, and to take risks. Multiple methods enable researchers to link past and present, 'data gathering' and action, and individual behavior with social frameworks. In addition, feminist researchers use multiple methods because of changes that occur to them and others in a project of long duration. Feminists describe such projects as 'journey's'... Shulamit Reinharz, 1992, Feminist Methods in Social Research. New York: Oxford University Press. p. 197

*Every culture has eyes and ears, as it were, and the woven
and beaded belts and blankets, the carved and painted
trays, the poles, doors, veranda posts, canes and sticks,
masks, hats, and chests that are variously part of many
oral performances among Aboriginal peoples, especially
those central to sacred or secular traditions... these forms
of writing are often just as important as the stories and
songs. Every culture not only sees things but also reads
them, whether in the stars or in the sand, whether spelled
out by alphabet or animal, whether communicated across
natural or supernatural boundaries...* J. Edward
Chambering, 2000, 'From Hand to Mouth: The Postcolonial
Politics of Oral and Written Traditions'. Reclaiming
Indigenous Voice and Vision. Ed. Marie Battiste.
Vancouver: UBC Press. p. 138

- JACQUELINE HOEKSTRA
- DANI PIGEAU
- ELLEN WINOFSKY
- MARIA WALTHER

JACKIE HOEKSTRA

"One is not born, but rather becomes a woman"
(Simone de Beauvoir).

As a poet, writer, researcher, teacher, and mother I lean into the interdisciplinary nature of my identity. I am who I am because of the intersections that exist in my work and my life. Because of my lived-experiences I understand and have worn some of the myriad faces of womanhood.

I single-parented my oldest son while attending college and university. I worked in the summers and parented during the school year on social assistance. Both poverty and my family taught me of the values of kinship networks. I learned an immeasurable amount about the strengths and stresses of writing, mothering, and friendship during these years.

My partner & friend, Boyd, provides support and his music adds fuel to the creative chaos of our lives. My two youngest sons were born while I was taking my MA courses and writing my thesis; they flavour the words that I wrote and the poems I created. My daughter was adopted last year at the age of two and came to live with us; she has taught me more about love, patience, and acceptance. The push and needs of my children brought me closer to an understanding of the importance of my mother and my women friends and mentors.

As a poet, my myriad experiences became both food and fuel. Teaching in Old Hazelton, Haida Gwaii, Terrace, Kitimaat, and Port Edward I was taught, in turn, by the women who attended my classes. They offered me other ways of knowing and other ways of looking at women, writing, and mothering.

My interests and goals are who I am and what I do. I mother, I write, I research and I cannot, will not, separate this from who I am as a researcher or as an academic. My goal, right now, is to devote a portion of my creative self to

SFU's English PhD program; this will enable me to formally pursue my cross-cultural research on mothering in B.C.

Thank you,
Jacqueline Hoekstra

.....

Secrets unkept

Have you ever seen a woman
fall to the ground cover her head in grief
make the noises a women makes in childbirth
call curses upon god and man, keen and moan
throw her limbs about madly
in vain to keep the certain dawning away?

Have you ever seen a women whose child has been violated
by the man that she loves, who whispered sweet words
in her ears she hears her daughter's voice telling her
how it happened that night when she was away working.

Have you ever cried torrents & rivers for the loss and the grief
and the anger that works its way up through channels and
gullies?
Has the anger risen within you until only the knowledge
of certain guilt that would follow stop you
from taking his pitiful life in your hands and squeezing make
back into clay
unform him, make him over?

Have you ever sat and held your best friend in your arms
and remembered how she and you too have kept your secrets
and shame for years ?
How the sins of the mothers will not fall upon the daughters
and love will climb the gates and the hedges will twine itself
around our
feelings till something green will grow
strong and we will say enough.
Enough.
It is enough.

....

For Sugar

The ghosts I keep
are reckless tonight
they spin and jitter, sashay and slide.
Fling head back and hip heavy.

Holding on with fingertips
the minimum of control
the occasional wince and shutdown,
eyes closed tight
leave them not gone but hidden.

Tonight they are hammer hammer hammering
at the front door, they call hey hey hey
dare me to unlock those bolts unhook the hasps
unbutton the hatches, they have been waiting long.

Looks on their faces, in easy chairs they sit
recumbent, redolent with memory
waiting for the next shoe to fall
the next icy finger to slide down my back
I was waiting too.

Do you remember when I wore red shorts
when my shoe laces were untied
when I played with my friends after school?
You were there, every little girl
when I climbed the mountain
when I tripped and fell
when you leapt from the bushes laughing
part of me still watching.
You were there.
Every little girl knows this fear.

Here you are again smiling easy
that no-big deal smirk.
Like lives haven't been lost

like little girls can learn how to trust
like trust can come back swimming
wagging its tail.

In the slow beat of red into red. Stolen.
You stole a piece of her
and shrugged.
Shrugged.

Shrugged like it doesn't matter
and the ghosts sing:
"watch out watch out "
because this time I'm angry.

Not lost, hurt, confused, ashamed afraid.
Angry, angry, angry
like the ghosts that shimmy in my head.
Watch us.

....

3 Gifts & holding
(teaching in Hazelton)

In the winter snows that settle or lay
heavy on the trees bowed
and bent with load

1- that coyote jumping over the barrier
   grey against grey
2- the broken lakeshore
   laps silver tongues against the black
3- rhythm of a crow's wing
   rifles the air clean and smooth.

It sounded like this: thrum, thrum, thrum.

So you tell stories
mock gently my white face
heads bent together laughter
smoothes the worries from your eyes.

Tell me about your father and your grandmother
their names and their faces
language keeps us company
my love and your love.

Our children

Travelling on these winter
visits on cold roads
listen closely
we find new patterns on the wind.

(for the wise women)
....

Cemetery Road

In my mind I am walking back
down old cemetery road.
The trees are overhung with old man's beard,
the remnants of this fence overgrown with moss so thick it
pillows,
you are not with me, though your memory is here.
Perhaps it lives here, your memory, on cemetery road.

Black ravens croak and call from the distant shore,
the road is grey sand and crushed clam shells.
I make no sound as I walk, there is only
the ravens and the ocean calling me through
this primordial forest, where
the markers of who was here remain.
Who we are
amidst the trees the moss the old man's beard

are the graves of settlers and people who began before we could
count.
These are the cemetery memories of you
your gentle voice, your smile
tilted sideways with unspoken questions you will always be here
on cemetery road.

.....

Sharon's classroom

Sitting in a coffeeshop in Haida Gwaii
I am waiting.
I am not good at waiting.
My eyes go to the crow wheeling free circles
in the blue outside.
Sharon's Aunt Mary is silent,
nodding her head a little to something
she can hear
Sharon is quiet also.

In this lunch hour Aunt Mary drinks Sprite
Sharon eats soup
I push around my food
I ordered too much, and cannot finish.

I watch the beautiful eyed children
think of my own, off this island
they seem very far away
I miss the way their bodies tether me.

I know there is something
I just do not get but
I am listening very hard to the silence.

.....

Going to Old Masset

You change,
misty-eyed and raven-locked
into difference
walking
floating
flying.

You enter,
nothing like the emerald
nothing like the basalt shores
of my iniquity, or yours,

Let us go then,
down this narrow waterway, where;
slate is not obsidian
obsidian is not argellite
argellite becomes the bones.

A framework for what has no reference
under his skin lie deep-finned sharks
under her skin anemone bloom in tidal pools.

There are no chalk boards
here I can only write
with my finger in the wake
of waves.

Forgive the marble hoax
here there are no intimations
no more Sunday school catechism

who is there to save?
This is the world where
the possibles of grey mornings
are not for grief but celebration.

.....

Mater Dolorosa

The heart of a lion when I was ten
clad in iron: caged thin and fierce
desperate and glad of
the dark side of justice.

Growing up on war stories,
Understood that right was right and to stagger was to fall.

Held grim council under countenance of darkness
promises promises: would never raise my hand to my children
never marry
a man like my father who: I couldn't speak.
Wouldn't find fear in my morning coffee wouldn't
hear my baby cry in the night and shout "shut up" "shut up".

On my knees in abandoned prayer I stare
at the bootstraps of that fervour; drink to my father's
alcoholic lease on joy. Know the thousand sins I have
committed in my heart and in my head, my hand itching my palm
leaking.

Father, Mother I stagger now
the daily tasks the bread the washing the milk teeth
smiles; I ache with my horrible love. I am done.

....

Maria

My mother,
with both hands held out
negotiates her path,
the potholes huge but not
insurmountable.

The planes of her la pays bas face

angle and decline.
Like the magi with gifts of
outlandish significance my mother gives
daffodils in yellow and red tulips,
held no resentment for sick children
flushed scarlet with fever
blonde with jaundice.

Pulling weeds in cabbage fields
we stopped when the sun was high
scorching us in the summer absences
with my father gone. Carried by her patience
In fields of ripe raspberries
the vermilion flash of
anger spent.

....

My father has fallen

Amongst the root vegetables
rutabagas, turnips, and spuds.
In this garden he was tall as the corn
unyielding as the alder supports
provided brace to grow up against.
We grew up against
his red words ran our tendrils
in wild directions.
Over the raspberry canes of his anger and out.

A good gardener provides direction but
has no need for carrots or peas to be
something else. Water melon does not growth this far north.
It lays green and yellow
small bitter balls that never ripen.

I find him now on his knees
searching for what he planted
over the years he has lost track of where

the cauliflower was allowed to bloom.
A kind of abandon took over.

Things grew green and brown and eventually yellow
coarse stalks brittle remnants
when he returned I think he knew
that it was too late for husbandry
what was wild stayed wild.

He is down among the rows now
attempting some kind of cultivation
the nettles hurt his fingers
and the thistles burn through
a crown of thorns for penance.
It is not enough for some of the vegetables
they are off in other pastures.
Still marked as my father's seeds.

......

In circles of Desiree

(circular logic for my daughter)

Nature hates a straight line
prefers bent wood boxes over stainglass precision
and so the serpentine cord of umbilica links us together.

Concentric circles lead from one beginning
into another.

The wings of the Tse Tse that fan a father's sorrow
in Burma cause the rain to fall upon a parched sharecroppers
land
and his children smile.

You are a part of who I am.

Your own plan

will in the end be as unmanageable
as mine, you are mine .

Like the totems that fall into forests of oblivion
created only for the moment and meant to return.
Like sandpaintings that say that the act of worship and creation
is enough,
intended only for wind blown hillocks.

The cold marble permanence of "I am forever" is
a hoax an elaborate jehovah.
You are my act of worship my creation of moment,
mutable and impermanent.

......

Carrier

Wolves nipping at your
heals for years
tear chunks of flesh, exposing
bone fragments splayed open and white
beneath your bruises blossom.

In bottles you find a retreat
behind the brittle years
every day so fragile
breaks into shards:
a small concoction, unguent of bliss
everything becomes bearable.

Bears, grizzlies, kodiaks, brunos
roam angry and childless
knocking into and through every day
damage done to your child-self; a cache
of punishment to dredge up
night-time stories to share over
burgundy or whiskey colors the sky
lovely golden-red.

Lies set down in strange pastures
bloom into beauty, even nature
believes in this holy love you trail.
They have your eyes;
your children are beautiful
only a hint of the pain remains
in their photographs
remains when you leave them.

You come back unexpectedly
like an early morning
Cat hauled and cat-licked you
are watching, only,
to make sure they are loved
you pick up and carry on,
somehow convinced
or faithful in knowing
your love is so strong it hurts.

Worship is still another word for forgiveness.

.....

Coriander on July 1st

We complicate our lives
by adding words:
Love, Need.

A longing for attachments
a frisson of tension
in the muttered endearments
we carry on
pick ourselves up from
the most unmentionable of circumstances:
Death, Abandonment.

The shade of the arbutus

forms columns on the sidewalks
we walk through
cold, hot, cold, hot

The shoulders of the Lady's mantle
are bright ocher in sunlight.

The cat's rough tongue
laps syrup from the empty plate.

, The top unstrung spins.

.....

Women Studies

Somewhere, in this moment,
texada island, hazelton, or tlell,
a woman is crying:
three women are crying.

They cry because they are lost or lonely or longing
for what they can not have:
love or children or bread to feed
hungry mouths, dry and bitter
sweet and sugary they are
and some cry for just a moment of release a moment where
they are the only ones to exist.

No babies crying for more milk
no children saying "look at me", "look at me"
no men with hard eyes and hands
to bring flowers to bloom upon your eyes
blue and green that fade to yellow.

Leaving only the pretty babies in
the afternoon sleeping, a moment where
they can love
these tied to the house/apartment/trailer
but not to the bed
posts of love.

.....

The Highway Song

> Her voice is like the edge of a knife paring
> carving flaying carrying feeding...

for Lee Maracle

It is the song that pushes us off the edge
past dredging up past misery
into an uncommon now
Singing in the half-light of the bar
wind in your lungs, laugh in our posture.

It is your song, you are singing.
We are listening.
The whole town hears you
in their sleeping
it is what we dream of all night long.
The sound of wind sweeping entire highways clean.

Past the what we know in the what we don't
here in a small-town bar
in small-town BC we are big
huge larger than our pasts
see it behind us: looming.

All of us women are here... women with sisters
mothers, daughters, friends.
New and shining, windswept
in this bar just before the Old Bridge
just past what used to be the Drive-in,
we sit together, loosened by liquor and song.

There is a trail from your highway song into
Patsy's highway song... a long line of women
walking... rolling earth beneath our feet
out in the moonlight
feeding our words into the window
of change of bridges bent from wood

and steel girdered to span deeps.

This song, this highway, these words
dropped like stone wishes off bridges
permanent and smooth
come from wind and mouths of change.

the last evening

for Eva

She spins god into her fingertips
feels his slick kiss
in the slurry oh her hand
buckets of fathomless deep.

Heavy, cold, and laden.

Ladles of new beginnings,
next to the spinning clay
she looses who she is, as,
she creates a cosmos
of need in grey tangibles.

That round and around
whispers god into the humming
strumming heel and toe against
baffle of wood.

Solid beneath her foot,
she pushes off into possibility
mixes elemental colours;

Guadeloupe blue mortars.
Pestle grinds her grey into stories
into impossible
luminescent births.

.....

DANI PIGEAU

Dani Pigeau is a student, a single-mother, an activist, and a First Nations cultural educator. She is Sto:lo, Haisla, and of Celtic descent. She came to writing as a way of transcending the bridge between herself and her ancestors. She feels that she sometimes has to go back in order to go forward with full authenticity and personal/ political empowerment. Writing is one way in which she expresses her concerns about the worlds she lives in. These are her first poems and she is pleased to have her "voice" heard in this publication. Speaking out is her way of connecting and ensuring the world is a better place for her family, friends, and especially her son, Estin. Dani was born and raised in Northern BC, and it is where she lives. She is currently attending the North West Community College.

Salvation Cakes [2]

Step one:

Repent all diadems with sickle, set a side

Step two:

Anoint uncircumcised lemons

Step three:

Heat embroidered maskil brethren to 250 degrees

Step four:

Swaddle satan's resurrection in virgin oil

Step five:

Add to chilled chrysolite idolaters

Step 666:

Mix all vigoursly, pour and let stand in sabbath deity until set and exile

---

[2] This poem is for all those struggling with the mainstream/ Eurocentric/ imposed religions. Finding our true spirituality is as simple as turning in and accepting what we find there.

Hedge is to horse [3]

Siting at a table that is not your mother's

Day Care: "Sit up Strait.. No elbows on the table.. Say excuse me"

"What do you call a baby horse?"

"Well that's wrong"

She chose hedge

Her mother works at a carpet factory.

"This test shows her I.Q."

Her head once FULL of BUGS, her father never FORGETTING.

Now being pressed full of WORDS with meaning.

"She is some what ready, but did not know what a baby horse was called"

"She should know, she's an INDIAN right?"

"I told her it's a colt"
"It didn't seem to register"

---

[3] This is a poem about my first memories of educational institutions. This piece of writing demonstrates the misunderstandings and racisms I encountered there.

BLANK STARE
ACCEPTANCE
SILENT STAND

"She should fit in to school just fine Mrs.........................."

"BUT, Please explain to her what a baby horse is called."

......

My Son Will See This [4]

Kacki trees on molded klay cliffs
Kleer kut youth

Shaded Sage
Kantean hollow whispers

Coded olive countenance

Mocked shag of mothers hair
Lifeless lank pestilence

Maggots breathe
Of life in ganggreen
Chard chambers of kacki

......

---

[4] This was written while thinking of mothers who watch their sons go off
to war. The horror in that watching resonates with me because I am the
mother of a son.

LIFE'S MOGULS [5]

SUNSHINE ON PARCHMENT
A YOUNG MAN STRIDES TOWARD ME
A RED GRIN FULL OF LAUNDRY

HE CARRIES MANY THINGS FROM YOUTH
OFFERING UP, OUT FRONT
DAMP, LIMP, WILLING REJECTION

EACH DEPRESSION A MOGUL OF BELONGING
ADDED TO ANNUALLY
CLINGING SICKLY TO THE SIDES
MOLD RIDDEN AND ROTTING

A FULL MOON SMILE MEETS MY GAZE
I SEE MUCH MORE GREY PILED HIGH BEHIND
THAT SMILE OF SOFT TEETH

HOLDING OUT RELINQUISHING ALL
SHORN AND BERIBBONED TO THE END OF KITE STRINGS
AS WHISPERED WINDS CARRIED TO CREATOR
FEATHERED RAGE FALLS AWAY

SETTLING THE RAGGED WET SLEEVES ONCE WORN
NOW ETCHED
SOFT SATIN SCARS ARE SEEN

...

---

[5] This is written for my friend Wilf. I want him to know that I hope he finds all that he wants in this life and that I thank him for sharing.

THE LIST [6]

BRAIDED BLACK HAIR
ROCKY SHORE
WARM SUN STREAM
UMBER HILLS (WITCH I STOLE)
SHATTERED BLUE SKY
LANKY LIME GRASS
BOBBING BURNT BOY
VEILED VIOLET VEINS

I SLEEP WHERE THE DEAD WALK.

......

IT'S LIKE <u>*YOU*</u> *DEAR ONE* [7]

STOLEN WORDS FROM BORROWED BROTHERS
EMPTY ARMS AROUND ME
A SCHIZOPHRENIC SQUIRRELS' PRAYER
A WAITING THAT NEVER COMES
BEING SORRY FOR NOTHING BUT EVERYTHING
KARMA LEFT UNDONE
BLUE GLASS SIGHING WRIST
SIGHS ONLY HALF SOUNDED
TENTATIVE BLISS
TEXTILE BRUISES
RAGE BRUSHED ASIDE
FOOD FROM THE FOUR CORNERS
LIKE RESPECT FOR A RAPIST
A THERAPIST ADDICTED
AN ABORTION UNDONE

---

[6] This is for my family and friends in Kitimaat Villiage. I thank you for all the gifts you have given me. I love you.

[7] Like Mother. Like daughter.

A ZEN RESPONSE TO YOUR CALL [8]

IN RESPONSE TO YOUR QUESTION
I FEEL MEEK AND SAVAGE

IN RESPONSE TO YOUR QUESTION
I FEEL RUDE I FEEL SMOTHERED

IN RESPONCE TO YOUR QUESTION
I FEEL COLD AND STAINED

IN RESPONSE TO YOUR QUESTION
I WILL SCRUB CLEAN THIS FEELING DOWN
MY DELIVERY WILL CHANGE

IN RESPONSE TO YOUR QUESTION
I WILL PATRONIZE YOUR STARE

IN RESPONSE TO YOUR QUESTION
I AM NOT EVEN HERE.

......

IT'S ME UNCLE ALFA [9]

IF ONLY YOU COULD SEE MY WAY, REALLY IT IS NECESSARY

IT TELLS ABOUT IT IN THE BOOK
I AM REALLY JUST A FRAIL PERSON SMALL OF STATURE

I HAVE KIND THOUGHTS, MY NIECE LOVES ME,
SHE SITS ON MY LAP
I SING SONGS AND DANCE

---

[8] To the authority, unknowing.

[9] My red hair and curls comes from the line of people Adolf Hitler tried to destroy. They are also my relations. This is written to Grandfather David Oppenheimer.

ME I TAKE CARE, ALL CLEAN AND NEAT

NOW BUSINESS, IS JUST THAT, IT IS NEVER PERSONAL
I KNOW THEY PLAY MUSIC
IT HAS TO BE DONE

STEP LIVELY KEEP TO YOUR TRUTH
HOLD FAST FOR WHAT YOU BELIEVE
LIFE'S FINALITY

GO OUT WITH A SMILE
DO IT FOR YOUR CHILDREN
IT WILL ONLY HURT FOR A WHILE

ALL WILL BE RECYCLED
WE WILL DISTRIBUTE WITH CARE
YOUR SKIN WILL RADIATE
YOU WILL ALWAYS BE NEAR

DON'T WORRY MIEN KAMPH
WE WILL TAKE PICTURES AND MOVIES
YOU'LL BE SEEN
                PROLIFIC
                    ANCIENT
                        A USED TO BE...

...

THE KEEPERS OF GRIEF
THE GREY MASTERS ELEPHANT [10]

GREY SHROUDS LIMP SKIN

SAGGING SADNESS' IN DROOPED COPPER LIDS

GREY GARGANTUCHIN POLES POUNDING IN UNISON

BRING THE WELL THAT IS RELEASED

IT IS THERE THE ANCIENT ONES SHARED THE SACRED

TURNING THE BONES OVER SMELLING OF DEATH

THE RED WAILS PENETRATE AIR

WE LEARNED FROM THEM WHAT IT IS TO REMEMBER

.....

---

[10] For those who need to claim the grieving – so that they might start living again.

OXCHA ROHO [11]

AMPLOSO

AMO

NINADA

PROBLIDAD

PENDULO

DOLORSO VERD

NACA

VERDE BLANCO POILO

RED WALLS

POMPOUS

BOSS

CHILD LIKE

INTEGRITY

PENDULUM

SORROWFUL GREEN

NEVER

GREEN WHITE CHICKEN

......

---

[11] This poem was inspired in response to a conversation about remembering our Grandmother's kitchens. It was painful to remember my grandmother's kitchen. I still miss her so much. This is for Kisa. My Swedish sister who spoke broken Spanish as well as I did, "Via con jhevious".

GIRRRR [12]

i think a minuet too late as you walk bye spitting the words
dog face! ANGRY trying to call me out, as i shrink TRYING to
ignore the hate overwelling in your words.

i sit with these words now and think smiling~ girrr if only my
response could have been quicker
i might have caused a riot...

i've FOUGHT these words in my mind, more comments linger
wagon BURNER, bug head. all sticky sweet, terms of endearment.
i WRESTLED them over and over in my mind, still i stand alone
looking at them, BRILLIANT red weeping shame.

you tell me, take ownership, call it your own half breed slowly i'm
coming to terms...... dog face ECHOES in halls of my mind. girr ,
well now i see the connection and BELIEVE me i WILL bend over
backwards trying to find how i fit, shaping molding my body to
this. finally breaking the mold i've been placed, so you know
you'll hear me saaaay fuck you

......

---

[12] This is for all the women who have been called UGLY...and as said so
well by Ani Defranco "Fuck U very much" to those who would demean
and diminish us!

it cripples me [13]

it cripples me, bending my back. splinters of shame from the others. black and blue untold unspoken. tears stream down, is that my truth or the truth of others the one they see. i only know it through a filthy window.

i prepare for the birth or is it a death. the deep shame walks with me daily, does it show? do they see it. guilt rapes me minutes, seconds out of each hour. time stands when i remember how you looked at me. i knew you were, i could feel it. am i a mirror for your hurts. do you want to comfort me or fuck me like the others. do your MORALS stop you or is it shame, well to want a squaw after all.

what is it like to reclaim the womb? i wonder, the warm pink comfort wet and pulsating with life. the pains are coming. sucking my breath back. i have to remember to breath.

it's time are you turned Its time i feel it. i can't prepare for this. will i burst when it happens will i lose you at birth or will i lose myself. i let go i beg for my FORGIVENESS so i can forgive the others, the ones that entered back wards trying to reclaim my womb backwards SLAMMING, thrusting into me trying to retreat.

they say it's our power place, the term one cord "connection"

i prepare for the coming time, i prepare for you

.....

---

[13] This is a poem to my lover who never loved.

once noticed [14]

spoken softly among the DELEGATES of the wounded,
it's your turn to step up and tell your story.
don't worry about were it GOES,
they all end up at the same place.
as you begin, it's slow and you waver
shyness takes hold as CONCERNED eyes rush you with
COMPLACENT...go on miss Reice.
near the end, slight tears are now VISIBLE,
the only REmNantS left behind of what they did.
you've cleaned up their mess, pretty GOOD. only three more
generations to go.
Thank you for your statement miss reice, they say as they walk
you to the door.

---

[14] This is for all the women who have been sexually violated and who
wanted to tell their truth – did tell their truth – but truth was disregarded
by the judges/ lawyers/ police/ the State.

ELLEN WINOFSKY

   This ain't your patriarch's poetry Book; Connections,
candles, comrades. . . was an exciting venture for Ellen, one
in which she could give tribute to the strength of
relationship. She strings together bobbles of words and
thoughts that have been enriched and encouraged by
special connections with people in her world. This necklace
of prose is dedicated to the wonderful souls who share their
lives with her. They mirror what in means to connect and
support, to build and challenge and rattle the bars of
patriarchy. Ellen can often be heard rattling through a
street-level, kitchen-table approach to activism. She

endeavors to detach from polarized either-or thinking and entices as much grey, sliver, shimmer and third space into her life as possible. She encourages dancing, splashing, crashing and scratching at/with the multitudes of possibilities to build and redefine relationship with Self and others.

She is **certain** that creativity is the key.
Ellen is a mother, social worker, artist, thespian and unformalized student of Feminine Psychology and Jungian Theory, . . She is a member of the Secondhand Theatre Company and dedicated groupie of Marion Woodman.
Ellen welcomes both the radiance and riotous confusion of connection and intersection with others and understands its impact on her bravery, bitchiness, competence, empathy, wonder and truth searching/telling.
Ellen has often been accused of talking too much, crying too long, laughing too hard, flying too high (or low), raging too intensely, loving too much, forgetting too easily, and bowing too deeply. To these charges she responds – I'm not done yet.

Ellen's fondness, admiration and gratitude goes to all her families, bio and chosen. With out them there is nothing. To Win, who's hung on for 25 years of stretching, scraping, challenging, laughing, loving, and growing into. To her four incredible children Morgan, Melissa, Michael and Mason, she remains intrigued and delighted at who they are as people. Their choices of comrades, their ability to plough through life being themselves, their empathy, thoughtfulness, brilliance and willingness to share and love so deeply.

To Colin, who matters for so many reasons, but mostly because he always got her and when he didn't, he wanted to. To Dee, because falling in love from across the room is so good for the soul, to Holli, always, always, always kindred spirit, to Margy and Jody for all the color, paint and creativity they bring to her life, to Terry and Corrina for the magic, to Rhonda and Joseph for spiritual guidance and push, and to Peggy, Patty and Kevin for all the formative loving and sharing, to Catherine, Ev, Kelly, Dorine, Brenda, Sherry, Michelle, Katy, and Jill, and many, many more remarkable people . . . for juiciness, support and humor. To the whole Winofsky crew for making the effort to stay connected. To Michelle Wasen for her talent and willingness to share her photographic eye and to capture the spirit of what she sees on film. To Maureen for starting a fire, to Heather for keeping it going and to Si for adding more fuel, much thanks.

To the multitudes of writers, artists, activists and the like who so selflessly paved the road and put up the down payment for the crown of freedom, equality and expression and all the people who realize this, support and wear the crown proudly by sharing their gifts and insights with the world – You have/are affecting us all in profound ways. Very special appreciation for her first family, Jim and Mary Koppari, Kathy, Steve, Jeannie, Beth, Tom, Kerry and all their amazing families. In spite of the great physical distance she is closely connected. She deeply thanks and loves you all – be well.

FRESH AND OPEN

It might as well be Spring
The inner creatures stirring
Parchment skin is shining
Heaving arms reaching
The earth is fresh and open
Welcome back my friend

.....

LEAH

Leah laughs when tears fall down
She sings when she is bleeding
She's torn the hair from her head
The garden needed weeding

.....

CLAIRE'S MOTHER

When Claire's mother was younger she often asked about her
father-- the shadow in her life, sensed but unknown. Her mother
would ear mark a page of her journal and pass it to Claire.
Reading thoughts.

Now the journal is left to her, the ear marker gone. Claire hears
the hums of solitude. She keeps the journal closed, deciding not
to read today, missing her too much.
Clair lifts the journal from the crumb covered table and with a
swoop of her arm the crumbs dance to the floor. As she set the
journal down a single loose page breaks free and floats,
crisscrossing in the still kitchen air, settling with the crumbs.
Clair reaches for the broom.

She sweeps the remnants of the last few weeks together into a
pile and sorts what should be picked up, put away, or thrown
out. She reaches for the journal page written by her mother's
then shaky hand--her last entry.

"Miles of discontentment lay at my feet.
How old was I when knew we are all running
from or to something?
How many lines of a song did I sing before
REALizing the melody?
How loud did I sing to hear my own voice.
how deep, how shrill?
How many prayers repeated on bending, wobbly knees
before understanding the significance of action? . . ."

Claire fills the dustpan and empties it into the garbage, holding
her mothers words in hand. Hearing the hum of her mother's
voice "I did what I could, I am not sorry".
The words resounding through her body, believable and
comforting.

.....

THE FIRST PICKING

The tightly woven basket
left a small faint welted mark
as it dropped to the table
tender green and gritty roots
nutrients from the Mother
overflowing container
weatHERed hands kissed with rich, dark
sweet feminine soil
pushing soft grey from
birch bark skin
revealing an enlightened grin
not the harvest
but the
first picking. . .

.....

LEMONAiDE BABIES

i too thought
of the youngest of women
earliest evidence and foreshadowing
the expanse of inborn spirit
and developing wisdom
reaping paragraphs
of strength

Lemonaide babies
inherent ability
to change
develop
quench
Primal determination
wishes and wants
rich with vision
and carry through.

.....

WHO-WE-WERE-THAT-MORNING

Remembering who-we-were-that-morning

Hearing   the holocaust stories

Recognizing
pieces of Self strewn
across the forest floor

Wanting
them back
not knowing
where they would fit

Reflecting
on who was preoccupied
and who was really focused

Pretending
we were all on the same page

Concluding
we may actually be
in different books.

The energy it took

Establishing
whether the situation was
improving or deteriorating

Embracing
the faint lines that don't pull apart
but hold through generations

Laughing
so hard we cried

Crying
so hard we changed the subject which

Shifting   us from

Who-we-were-that-morning   ReMEMBERing. . .

....

FLESHING OUT

Fleshing out
stretching
past the skeletons
adding meat to bones
Bones
of ideas
of gratitude
of awe
of scars
of scares, dares and awares.

Fleshing past
initial presentation
how we are
who we are
what we are
where we're from
and how much we
Carry
Disown
Discover
Realize and
Remake.

LADDERS FOR EACH OTHER

When women dance with flames
They become the fire
Lasting energies
Herstories etched in barkless flesh
Ladders for each other
Tracking miracles
From crystal ships
To catch those dangling
Visiting the mist
And clearing skies
Illustrated everyday in the
Portraits of strength
Beautifully written portraits
A universal language
Guiding us on.

....

YOUR MY OUR

brilliant
tender
nagging
craving
broken
building
wise
warming
tattered
wonder
widening
loving
dropping
credible
capable
radiant
rich
remarkable

SELF

....

MARIA WALTHER

The day I joined a women's group for the first time in my life – however challenging it proved to be - was the day I began the long, pain-filled journey home towards my own healing self: in the company of supportive friends.

Since then, I have worked in the areas of music, mothering, farming, ecological feminist activism, and language. On

many occasions, my precarious sense of selfworth
threatened to shatter and disappear in the misogynist
minefields of a capitalist patriarchal culture – and always, it
was the dawning of feminist consiousness that moved me
beyond valleys of depression, beyond the viscious cycle of
abuse, even beyond the schizophrenia of a split immigrant
identity.

And like all women, in the precious company of friends we
carry on together - we carry on, we collaborate, we
strategize, our multiple experiences converge at cyber speed
into a sacred maze of energy, commitment, and sheer good
will; we are the women standing in line at the Ministry for
families and children; we are the lovers, sisters, mothers,
daughters, friends and neighbours; we are all of those and
we help each other retrieve our selves each day to step forth
into the light of collective honoring. Each small step
another link. Each link a beginning. We celebrate
togetherness, physical and spiritual sustenance, we grow
ecstatic over small gestures and large embraces – through
all challenges we thrive and keep on questioning and
digging: we are resilient, gorgeous survivors.

These then are the questions that continue to move me as
we head into the new millennia: How do we continue to
initiate and carry on the multivocality of an ethics of care
seven generations down the road and in the process lose
neo-colonialisms? how do we do this as committed allies of
all disadvantaged peoples, permanently dissolving
boundaries while celebrating unique diversity in culture
and self? how do we continue to do this collaboratively in
song, dance and re~affirming ritual? how do we do this as
earthbound women & men & children together, respectfully
supporting each other & all forms of life with~in~through it
this our earth? how? my guess is one haphazard step at a
time... For now I see us linking hands and spirits

everywhere as bearers and caretakers of a controversial &
frivolous species; what matters is the lush ground we may
continue to walk on. sway hips feel earth. touch earth
cradle soil. with y-our strong:soft callused feet of many
shapes and shades. y-our feet. unbound.

friendship: to Cindy

how we met on that
unlikely early summer evening
in the lush heart of summerland okanagan
the name says all
how I still see your small figure engraved
in the white door frame that
like a passive opening
seemed to hold you in abeyance
neither swallowing nor releasing you   .
deferring you into the dark silhouette of female still-life
who waits to resume a task she has yet to find
fulfilling.
as yet there is no light streaming out from behind you
the way blond novels promise
only the sterile white door frame nailed to a
vast anaemic surface that escapes meaning
whose unlived-in façade presumes
only
smooth mortgage payments.
I remember your quiet poise
a stillness that held your softly outlined body
like permanence though unresolved
like glimpsed imprints of past joyous movement
polished then stilled into forgetting
yet
waiting to resume
life.
what happened next
the children and I spilled into your driveway
your body gathered self
stepped outside the hold to allow your dog
eager greetings
strands of your hair unhurriedly mingled with the warm breeze
sun entered
your eyes flowed into your gentle smile
conversation began
movement remembered

this picture turned colour
for ever.
how my spirit fell in love with yours
at this moment before the pastoral openings of
sweeping meadows and hills before the fragile dignity of
your too slim person who I pray for
greets her own brave stubborn
bodys~pace.

....

a m/other escape
or
domestic refugee

sings to her raw heart beating: small cradlesong home
throughout
a stranger's winter
seemed to pull us each day closer
towards the muffled edge of a waning town
towards the wide mongolian plain of
superimposed pause
its alien selfcontainment
its disappearance of home-stead(y)ing syllables

and then made to
witness the quiet
humming of low temperature
that slowly
fell
below arctic whalesong
below children's heart ache
even below my caring and
shifting of daily purpose
in efforts to remember be~long~ing
as (if) it mattered

for seven months (almost full term)
we lit candles and huddled
inside our makeshift shelter
pressed into rambling coherence
by furious remembrance and
memory bundles
kept all doors locked as if to
protect a stranger's composed darkness outside
from intimate tormenting nightmares
within

now
on a transient's blossoming verandah
I look up from my readings into the
sundappled moments that become
animate children
streaking through and
out of last winter's demeaning
into the midsummer's spirited fest

now
after a tendril of green spring
we cautiously reach out and
claim home shelter
inside the amazon wilderness of our
back yard that wilfully spawns whole neighborhoods

in the deft circles of two dozen flower pots
that push against worm-eaten railings
their serene terra cotta smiles
giving away nothing
beyond dreams of stark longing
that pulse through my midsummer night

& although now barely past noon
into this shimmering blue summer arc
a slow darkening grows
near my heart
in that vacant region

where my womb lived
where now lies the promise of
a life alone

unmolested.

coming out female: where can friends meet
where can friends meet
but in the vacancy of her dreams
lost to the guardianship of public decorum
lost to His private eye

we will say I love you to a stranger
and mean it
feeling such keen pleasure
such acute sense of freedom
like a spare set of lungs
full well knowing sensuality this fluid thing
this
    shimmering of body streams
flowing flowing

.....

motherdaughterbreathing

(reflection on recent conversations with my mother)

if at times in our polished conversation-ceramics syllables seem
to shake
        loose
        hurdling sound fragments into/through fuming
afterthought
        -off chance meaning?

usually   with every breath we announce
        closure
with every line of barren small talk we continue to
        listen away   forever
forever cancel what we just
said and   really   how
we meant

at the end of each visit
and as usual
our solitudes collapse with the fatigue of deliberate misreadings
like controlled hugs hastily dropped in passing
among polite strangers
not quite a waste
but brittle
easily shattered

throughout as usual
we struggle into breath wheeze   gasp
each crowded breath we catch
lock in with the quiet fierce panic of the dying
quick shallow gasps we suck from deep below our rib cage
in a knotted space tightly contained away from our selves
because
a spillage would fill our throats
fill them with endless life
fill them with memories that boil to the surface
        hot purposefully alive

pungent and keen like fermented compost
or foaming yeast

and just as potential
until now we have managed our pain
like feet bound   to please
our screams sucked back and like dried blood peeling away our
throats
and as our hips quiver indefinitely and sweat never appears
under our armpits
shoulderblades push back heave upward   stick out
manoeuvre these carefully staged breasts - in order to look the
part with every breath

we suffocate -

          - yet
          as of late   after all these years listening
          listening   past
          layers lift   loose with desperation

                    and
                  meaning
                  becomes
                    as
          in the middle of long prayer
                  suddenly
              without warning
            like a flash of unwanted
          alarming insight that once released
              requires permanence
        and heals into the impervious boldness of a
              puckered scar

                  now
after all these years rituals of listening away conveying nothing
              now that she is alone
        a never before curiosity in her newborn gestures
              reaches for her smile

(calm even)
and as I watch my mother rise and
quietly unwrap
from the corners of her eyes
quietly unfold
her body
memory into a distinct
sigh
enter
motherdaughterbreathing

.....

explorers

some times   and more
when the waxing moon pulls our scattered memories
and our periods remember
we reach far

far back to an away oasis   where joy
and other soft beginnings
nestle together in the dampness
between our musing breasts
when curves
landscape deep-throated watersheds
arch mountain tops gasp cave hollows
and pour fertility waves into seasonal essences
like flirting summer breezes and
unhurried pregnancies
gaze fondling gaze
until hands
now luminous with love
roam gently among pubic hair
carrying all spice and innocence

no panic
only
the gorgeous birthing
of
female delight.

....

medusa

At times
the world rains sibyls and other
small creatures of the strange
- don't know what I would do
without their promiscuous laughter
as they chase all my preconceptions
as they beckon me into their voluptuous space
whose throbbing sometimes even I can feel
Inside their nonchalance I will move to be
long ago   where
lived with a wise woman whose frothy hairdo
even for those times is
shall we say - a bit on the riotous
and her perceptive smile we know so much about
(the smile he fears) so what
her petsnakes,
lovely bunch all glistening orange and lemon peel,
who secrete ovaries and
copulate habitually,
babble soft secrets into the luminous folds of her large
mother-of-pearl ears
secrets that turn her on
for ten thousand years

still turn me on
whenever I listen
into my own
song

when ever I sing.

.....

resolve

winding themselves around
lilies my name
even the trees suggest elaboration
a new year's wish
barely audible
nonetheless
          wisps of grey hair sticking out
reminder of a
stubborn
will

.....

on your own terms women: let me know each of you

in truth
shall i ever know you
know you the way you trust your self just so
surviving within yours
outside my markings

shall i ever commit all efforts
needed that convince you
i care
beyond a feminist blush

in my dreams
my body steps closer to yours
in my dreams
while yours keeps bending
my body bends down with you
wordlessly we collect firewood
a bit of harvest
dried dung
together we may set out on the daily five mile walk
to collect clean water
do washing in the sewers nearby
the Ganges
or a pure mountain stream
grind corn
play with our children
laugh with them
teach them
give birth to them
walk our bodies through the crucial necessities in
your life that also becomes mine
when i dream of you

and
when i dream of you
i see your face
and feel your body
bend only slightly away from me
as of late
we are so close in my dream
i smell the sweat on your skin
and know that at least that has changed
that into my waking hours
i am also learning to sweat
under the rising moon of consciousness

if
words
must fall

let me ask you this

have we entered a moment
in which you can even stand to hear me say
that i want to
am learning to resign
my role as accomplice in this colonizing evil
that i want to
and will find ways to honor
what you know
has always been yours
and feel
that you and i and she and she may
side by side
settle down our different selves
limp
in mutual
splendid ease

.....

:out of the past and into distinct possibilities

a woman's hopes
are many and long lived
that her body not disappear
that her partner could be her lover
that someone be her lover
a love be welcomed
that between her tears and her laughter there be no hate
that this her love for all life not be madness
and if she is
that they won't pierce her body in a quest for no blood

that one day
an immortal will step out and declare herself
or shut us up
that poetry always be like dream's trembling sigh

caressing our softer borders
that tomorrow will grow organic
and the air turn blue again
with curiosity and forgiveness
that this night be danced in and made bearable
and her family sleep well into a connectable future

a woman's fears are many and outlived only by her dimpled hope

.....

2. CANDLES (PRESSING LIGHTLY INTO THE PAST/ PRESENT/ FUTURE)

Two or three things I know for sure, and one of them is how long it takes to learn to love yourself, how long it took me, how much love I need now. Dorothy Allison. 1995. Two or Three Things I Know for Sure. New York: Penguin Group. p. 67

In the Thirties we did not know the term 'cultural shock.' The phrase reached me long after I had reached the West Coast. Language must have evolved like that! And how much clearer is the experience, in your mind, when you can name it. Is this perhaps the main reason for becoming a writer? Dorothy Livesay, 'The West 1936', (1977) Right Hand Left Hand. A True Life of the Thirties: Paris, Toronto, Montreal, The West and Vancouver. Love, Politics, The Depression and Feminism. Don Mills: Musson Book Company. p. 182
.....

We don't know precisely how, and that's not really
important. We know that the notion of power and its use
would be transformed; we know that the substance of what
is valued would be transformed. But since none of us know
the capacity of women freed from centuries of enslavement,
none of us can demarcate the route or conceive the end
result of such freedom. There is no one way feminism on this
road.
  We're up against the world, literally, if we want to
change... Marilyn Waring, 1996, Counting For Nothing:
What Men Value and What Women Are Worth. New
Zealand: Allen and Unwin, p. 257

You must write, and read, as if your life depended on it...
     To read as if your life depended on it would mean to
let into your reading your beliefs, the swirl of your
dreamlife, the physical sensations of your ordinary carnal
life; and, simultaneously, to allow what you're reading to
pierce the routines, safe and impermeable, in which
ordinary carnal life is tracked, charted, channeled...
Adrienne Rich, 1993, What is Found There: Notebooks on
Poetry and Politics. New York: W. W. Norton and Company.
p.33

- *SI TRANSKEN*
- *LYNN BOX*
- *THERESA HEALY*
- *YOLANDA COPPOLINO*

SI TRANSKEN'S

INEVITABLY INTERSECTING AND COMPLICATING IDENTITY PEGS

photo courtesy of Dr. Marianne Gosztonyi Ainley

Si has been involved in facilitating/ encouraging/ editing/ writing six creative books of non-standard commentary. In these experimental spaces she can vent/ celebrate/ heal and do mock-umentary. She has also published her poetry and prose in a variety of other locations (Canadian Women's Studies, Canadian Dimension, Perspectives, Reflections On Water, Azure). She has her work preserved in more than a dozen dry serious

sober scholarly forums (some of which might be defined as
more "Real" in that they were "Refereed Journals" or
chapters of anonymously peer reviewed books such as
Caring Communities; Care and Consequences; Feminist
Utopias; and Auto/Biography in Canada). Since 1960 she
has been trying to resist being in a bad mood. The more she
knows about the unfairnesses of this capitalist/
patriarchal/ corporatist/ racist world the more irritated and
impatient she is and the harder it is to perform the public
display of being a gentle cheerful person.

She is a gracefully militant advocate of Discipline-
Jumping (Social Work, Creative Writing, Women's Studies,
First Nations Studies, Sociology... + ++ +...). She is an
elegantly militant advocate of Genre-Jumping (seeking out
and mixing the knowledge to be found in testimony AND
scholarly writing AND poetry AND diary writing AND
journaling AND oral herstory AND grafitti... + + +...). In
regards to the truths of the lives of vulnerable populations/
subalterns Academia is often the last place to offer any
depthful useful integrated knowing! Participating in these
kinds of self-publishing collectives is very exciting to her
because she believes that all our voices can find themselves
in their own organic truths and be shared in our own
unique modes of expression. The authors in the **This Ain't
Your Patriarchs' Poetry Book; Connections, Candles,
Comrades** collective awe her. They continue to take risks
every day by being truthful; by exposing their frayed hearts;
by trying to make the world around them an improved
place. These outrageous acts of kindness are undertakings
they usually do with minimal resources and
encouragement. Si wants it known that she feels privileged
to witness the truth telling/ and fiction-centered
explorations of the other people in this book.

Si is an unashamed knowledge junkie! She's an info-slut! She'll pick up or lie down with insights from any street corner or from any everyday ordinary context. Her twenty years of social activism; work as a therapist with women who've experienced violence; her own healing journey - these eclectic 'classrooms' have sincerely and complicatedly **educated** her. Although she has completed her doctorate in Sociology/Equity Studies (and has many additional diplomas and certificates) she is enthusiastically committed to now completing an M.A. in Interdisciplinary Studies at UNBC in First Nations Studies and Creative Writing. All of the above dimensions of who Si is and what she cares about could be concisely communicated by saying she is **an honorably confused Cultural Studies Un/Scholar**. She has been teaching in social work programs for six years and is thrilled with the encouragement and affirmations she's received here at UNBC from peers, students, social work comrades, and courageous ordinary people in the community of Prince George.

THE POWER & THE GLORY! [15]

i've had the bone-growing privilege:

to teach with those who come to each lesson
creatively & effectively prepared;

to learn with women who quest for knowledge
beyond marks, scores, or game winning;

to ponder with those who light candles for others
stuck in dark spaces;

to strengthen with women who lift weights,
push limits, break mirrors, kick down walls;

to organize with those who have vision
& share it usefully;

to comrade with women who are beyond bullshit,
sniveling, scab picking, snot prizing...

to sit with those at meetings who accomplish
precisely what they promise they'll do;

to march with women who soulfully know

---

15 There are hundreds of women who have influenced my sense of self!
These women have taught me about the women's movementS and about
how to BE a women's movementS. And with each project I engage with I
try to thank the most recent contributors to my courage. Some of the
ones that I want to mention here include: Marianne Gosztonyi Ainley,
Dawn Hemingway, Jacqueline Baldwin, Margrit Eichler, Roxana Ng,
Sandra Acker, Kitty Minor, my writing peers in many women's circles,
Antonia Mills, Judith Lapadat, Julia Cameron, Keith Louise Fulton,
Barbara Issac, Barbara Herringer, Morgan Gardner, Diana Gustafson,
Arlene Herman, Heather Peters, Jeanette Turpin, Julie Lebreton, Mary
Fournier, Melanie Robitaille, Phyllis Parker, Shelley Latreille, Shareen
Ishmael, Linda Muzzin, Karen Benge, Leslie Bella, Laurel Richardson, the
students who share their wisdom with me...

why we put one foot in front of the other;

to contemplate with those who share wisdom
from their now-healed hurts;

to be with women who invest in their deep-selves
not just makeup or room decor;

to read with those who claim
space, resources, time to become epic;

to theorize with women who comprehend connections
across generations & diversities;

to reassess with those who see so much outside,
inside & before themselves;

to forward with women who are tired of dumping
their puss & piss on other women;

to advance with those who are tired of having
someone's piss & puss dumped on them --

to be blessed with all this. i have witnessed revolutions
& awed at how worlds can change over & over again
within even one conversation.

.....

KNOCK OUT BEAUTIFUL

> *...there is luminous rage & effervescent sweetness
> on this uncatwalk where storebought teen models fear to
> tread...*

5'3" & 122 pounds amassed
mostly against disasters & diminishments
(those of my peculiar dramas

& those of the vaguely anonymously defined
oppressed masses).

scraggly straight red rag-doll hair
above a deliberate &
anti-doll indelicate brain.

strong lashes, sassy black eyes gazing
ahead sideways backwards
& most importantly, mostly, inwards.

nose bridged with a bump
from confronting a crowbar's
explosive confidence
cuz it had won battle with a rusty nail.

dentists' families
have been economically dependent
on the production
& reproduction of
level unpained whiteness
in my mouth; those investments
have crafted a smile
that ricochets back.

frown lines, freckles, large pores,
laugh lines, a brow defined
these days by days which are too long
& have been for too long.

a voice that might have
promoted me to phone-porn queen
if i could contain my giggles
& contempt.

there is unstoppable unspeakable beauty in me
when i make even all this
make the world
come together into something
ironically laughable.

.....

THERE & HERE MOMENTS & PLACES

Constance, a childhood bestfriend taught
about resistence.
she'd found that skill by pushing back brothers -
one of whom had killed.
later, she took to wearing leather
& loving wifely women.

Kristy, kissed me lots lots lots
hard long low in the barn. she taught
about running. she never came back from Toronto.

Teena, was a diva who taught
about rough roads.
she topped fear with toughness & rocked gently
when we were alone but in public she sliced away sweetnesses.
she died of AIDS.
sex trade work didn't deliver
much magic in our boom/bust mining town.

Kathy, didn't notice
how i followed her waiting for attention.
she taught
about easy boundaries & smart laughter.

Those profs i dreamt of -
teaching me
explicit lessons
& of hearing more about special moments & places...

Always the sly malesteam world
pulls desires into their tidy con
cock ed easier flow; teaches me
where i belong in the allegedly
pre-ordained formula.

This lover now
i ride like Teena; wear leatherspirits for; run with.
we laugh a lot at smart stuff.
he understands the pull of
she moments & places.

.....

SURRENDERING TO
SELF-CRIPPLING

incessantly, frenetically, disturbingly
we mull the riskriskrisk of:
leaving mates we don't love,
quitting jobs we dislike,
severing un-nurturing friendships,
rejecting mean relatives,
disrupting unwholesome circles.
better to have the dulldreary of something/someone
than be our selves
in quivering fullness & questing growth.

pathetically, obsessively, tragically
we fear the riskriskrisk of:
spending on our education,
investing cash in our creativity,
rewarding our curiosity,
writing cheques for our boldwhimsy
dollaring at our playfulness.
better to put resources on

children/ mate/ pension plan
& a new Sear's couch.

- one ended relationship
one screech of the word **NO**
one week's wages devoted
to forwarding private goals –
one week of truly being our solid selves
from thousands of weeks of existence –
this kind of self-kindness
is embracing more terror
than almost any of us
can confront.

so when we witness that exquisite woman
who left/ concludes/ quits/ stands up / is seen
giving more than a week &
more & more & being
wildly big & saying **NO** as it suits her
(the one who refuses martyr-ing into extinction)
as it extravagantly suits her
 -- her existence nags & haunts us.
to even be seen at her side
is to riskriskrisk...

.....

BROAD SIDING

i don't identify with patriarchial faiths'
but they say a **Judas**
is a person who betrays a friend.
perhaps related to that original narrative:
a **judas hole** is a peep-space in a door.

irrelevantly & irreverently the
judas tree displays
enticing purple flowers

before it grows
small indifferent leaves.

my faith resides in solidarities &
potentials for kindness.
doors all round open, close, offer viewing spaces.
any tree any where unfolds itself
in the order destiny impels.

unrelated & irrelevant to each other are
women who've betrayed me
in tiny boring ways.
there have been many; their sticky petals,
their scent, their leavings untidy.

there seems to be one trying
to gaze into my center & sink
vampire roots
at any twist or time. mother was
the original narrator of this identity.

my pride grows in that i nurture
them much less now;
notice them more fleetingly,
surround myself
with lush foliage & strong doors.

faith resides in my growing ability
for finding faithful spaces
& strongwomen who know
about deeper roots & multiple ways
to unfurl powerfully lovely selves.

.....

FOR/ TO/ IN
RESPONSE TO LEE MARACLE'S WRITING [16]

i want to say **i know**
how you feel but that would be a lie;
stealing, minimizing, self-aggrandizing.
something
vital & central might be taken.

i want to say **i'm sorry, forgive us**
but i know this is shallow, hard to swallow
something felt like
nowhere
near enough for today; for building
affinity & empathy for tomorrow;
certainly not enough
to non-implicate me
in mainstream histories/ herstories.

i want to say **i hope**...
but i know this isn't enough; we're both
busy, tired, nervous, vulnerable
differently
hustling for protections, bandaids, proteins.

i want to say **it's not my fault**

---

[16] I thank Lee Maracle for facing, overcoming, speaking out about so
many challenges. Her writing describes experiences that no one should
have to encounter. I feel humbled, shamed, intrigued - and a few
thousand other emotions - as I read her semi-autobiographical material
such as Bobbi Lee and Daughters are Forever. I also feel admiration and
optimism while I witness how resilient, effective, courageous and
intelligent she is in her writing/ way of being. My respect and affection go
also to Barb Waterfall, Teena Lacoste, Fanny Eshkagogan, Catherine
Baylis, Susan Freeland, Dee Horne, Louise Erdrich, Marie Battiste,
Margo Greenwood, Barb Hume, Julia Emberly, Susan Fletcher, Chrystos,
Paula Gunn Allen, Patricia Monture-Angus; and many students/ peers/
activists/ clients for educating me about the things I need to know/
things I need to do/ person I want to become.

don't be mad at me
get over it but i know my white skinned
nonReserved life trajectory,
layers of loss
are less layered, less
loss full, less long.

i want to say **let's be something funny**
casual, comradely, calm
but i know emergencies, horrors, griefs,
urgencies lurk
all around us
& around our un-us-ness.

i want to say i'll listen while <u>you</u> talk
but i know my mouthy-mind has been socialized
to clutter-up & clutter-down
spaces between strangers.

i want to say **i'm side stepping**,
stalling & dis
connecting; falling on
old centers, binaries, edges, borders
unknowns but i know
i'm not good at contradictory authenticity.

i want to say **i know how much i don't know**
but confessing
absences & voids
disorients, frightens, weakens me.

i want to say **i do know that**
our
interactions should not be a ramble about
my unsorted
sort-of-Settlered
wants anyway
but...

i want to say **it's been a long wait**
& still language/ skin/ land/
spiritual stances
are signboards for hate -
but i don't know
the best whowhenwhere
for wording all this.

.....

Not mentors. Everyday Amazon-guides.[17]

our scholars
who now raid graves, rise up brilliant lost voices;
shine the brilliance in the voices
of their formal & accidental students;

our poets
who now revive our hearts
after so many landslide unvictories,
homicides, suicides;

our activists
who now turn back the 1001 Big Lies &
turn out revised theories,
turn up volumes on our truths, turn millions of lives around;

our researchers
who now questingly dive
again, again, again into the numbers/ charts/ pages
directed against us;

our entrepreneurs
who now donate to causes; who don't distress

---

[17] My wildest gratitude goes to Amazons like bell hooks, Adrienne Rich,
Marge Piercy, Susan Griffin, Dorothy Livesay, Dorothy Parker, Judy
Chicago, Emily Carr....

their workers; who don't sell
every portion of every person for profit;

our artists
who now (while forced to live like refugees
in their own lands) still put magicsoul
into our bruise-weary geographies;

our achievers
who now make it to some kind
of safety, a front line, a place of truth
& who reach back & forward & help others;

our comrades
sisters mothers friends neighbors
coworkers daughters; our natural resources growing the world
differently & undangerously

our whole beings
hurt when we now hear anyone say
that the feminist movements are unnecessary
& dead.

.....

LYNN BOX

Working in the banking bastion of patriarchal capitalism for twenty plus years taught me well the benefits of power and oppression. And yet, at some level I knew that I too was oppressed - although I would not/could not articulate this notion. Not an uncommon position for those with limited power but enough power to be part of the oppression of others. Being immersed in women's studies and gender studies for the past ten years has provided me, not only with the feminist language to describe patriarchy and oppression, but also the tools to possibly affect change. It is my hope that through participation in this project I may contribute to feminist solidarity. The major part of my contribution involves reflections about my great-grandmother/Madeline Izowsky/Gammie. She lit candles so that my life could be warmer, brighter, and more luminescent. My connections with her generation are visible in my comparative wealth of opportunities, resources, and choices. Writing about her belongs here in a book that celebrates that we ain't in as much of a patriarchal world as she was in ... when she was my age. Determining strength from my foremothers to recognizing kindred feminist spirits in the present remains a delight/an oasis/a thirdspace/ place of renewal and inspiration for me.

Feminism means finally that we renounce our obedience to the fathers and recognize that the world they have described is not the whole world. Masculine ideologies are the creation of masculine subjectivity; they are neither objective, nor value-free, nor inclusively "human." Feminism implies that we recognize fully the inadequacy for us, the distortion of male-created ideologies, and that we proceed to think, and act, out of that recognition. (Adrienne Rich, 1977, p.xvii)

PAST:

In honour of my great-grandmother:

My great grandmother, Madeline Izowsky (Gammie), came to
Canada from Poland in 1898. Originally pioneering in Alberta,
and the Crowsnest Pass area, she subsequently moved to Prince
George where, alongside her husband John, she raised four
children, helped build, in a strong entrepreneurial spirit, several
businesses, and provided matriarchal leadership for her family
until her death on December 19, 1979. Gammie's legacy of love
and strength has passed down through the generations of women
(and men) in our family. While recently writing a feminist
biography of her life, I became aware of how important she was/is
to my notion of who I was/am. I think it is important that her
words speak as much as possible and, therefore, the following
excerpt is a bricolage of an interview with Madeline Izowsky in
1971, selected parts of letters to various family members, and my
memories, which give a brief peek into this wonderful woman's
life. You will recognize her words as they are in bold italics.

***November 25, 1971 ~ I'm only going to be 87 and I'm glad I
still get around. I eat good, I sleep good, and I sit good.
That's all I can ... But Prince George is to me really home.
I've been here 57 years.*** Imagine how fortunate I was to have
this wonderful woman in my life for 27 years.

Spring, 1898 ~ Madeline Izowsky was ***12 ½ jears ol and come
to thes countre Canada and went to Polish scohl ther.*** There
were ***starving taym wen was en Polant.*** Imagine how difficult it
was to leave friends, grandparents, and other extended family
members, to travel to a different country/different
landscape(s)/different life. Madeline's family originally settled in
Round Hill, Alberta where they ***lived on the farm, and we
would farm and we had lots of nice fruit. You know went to
dances. We used to come in and take the accordion in. We
had sleigh riding and winter fun and gather up with
neighbors and have lovely party when I was young. We had
lots of fun. We use to ski and skate and things like that. We***

*learned to skate outside on our own and ski and snow rides
and sleigh rides. In those days took the horses and sleighs
and we just went miles and we had a good time. You know.
And the same way after we got married. Well we lived
thirteen miles from home we used to take the sleighs, we
had the horse and sleigh, and we took the sleigh and the
kids and hay in the wagon with hot bricks so they would
keep their feet warm. The horses took a while to walk,
especially when it was cold. We always had to be home for
Christmas. I think the kids were just as good as now, I think
they had lots of fun here but we had just as much fun then.*

November 21, 1904 ~ After her marriage to John they moved to
various mining towns in Alberta and British Columbia. Imagine
what it was like to leave her family, friends, and familiar
surroundings (again) to travel to different towns/different
landscape(s)/different life. It was during these travels that she
became a mother of four. They finally moved to Prince George
*because it was open up the country and everybody was
raving about it was going to be booming. We had a home
and property in Camrose and my husband decided to come
and see what the country was like so we come up and he
liked it a lot. He bought a lot. We paid $1,400 cash for one
lot, couple years after we bought another one in a tax sale
for $70, so it just shows you how town was booming and
then it went right down during the depression.*

May 1914 ~ Family history recounts that when they arrived
Madeline was terribly disappointed at the lack of a town and she
sat on a stump and cried. Imagine what it was like with nothing
but mud in the streets, no place to do laundry, no familiar friends
or family, and only her small children for company. A different
town/different landscape/different life. *When we come here in
1914 in May, it wasn't much of a town, mostly big stumps,
no streets, no sidewalks, and there were quite a lots of
people come in living in shacks or tents and building homes.
Well it was just 7th Avenue here, there were no sidewalks, it
wasn't graded, it was just grass and that and 3rd Avenue*

was the same way. We didn't know where the street was going to be.

We built quite a good size building, which we started a grocery store, and we lived in the back and we had two rooms upstairs. When we were first here we had a cow, we had a horse to haul the groceries, we had chickens and we even had geese. One year we got all the way down to Fort George, went and got four geese eggs and put them under the hen and so we had four ... three geese and the next year we kept those and the year after we had six and then after that we had eighteen and mind you we didn't sell one and we had a goose every Sunday for dinner. They were all right to eat, I would say.

Fall, 1914 ~ Education of her children was important to Madeline and as they had left a new school in Camrose she was disappointed that there was no school in Prince George for the children to attend when they arrived. The situation was soon rectified and *in the fall they started a school, it was a building, a rooming house, on the third avenue across the street from where the tennis court is. The bigger children started at school, which I have a boy Charlie, 9, other 7, he went to school but the other two there was no room for them. And then in the spring they built three little houses up here on First Avenue. In each little house has a two rooms and this was quite a nice school. Well, finally they built a school, which is still standing on 7th Avenue and Winnipeg Street. That was the best school that we had and those days they had up to grade twelve, which I think the children did just as good those days as they're doing in those big schools they have now. And my children passed grade twelve. So that was our schooling.* Imagine what it was like to not have English as a second language programs, mother's allowance, unemployment insurance, and social assistance in times of financial stress.

Then in the fall of 1914 the war broke out ... the first war broke out ... things weren't bad ... till about a year after the young people that come in here and started out. They knew they had to go to war the young men or starve ... there was no work for them. They couldn't get a job for 25 cents an hour so they just ... part of the young people moved away. The young men went to war and the wives they went back to live with relatives or went to England with their husbands. Then that was very bad depression for about two years and then after that things started picking up after that. The sawmills started up, the streets started work, Prince George houses started building.

1930s ~ Their activities centered on family, neighbors and community. *Well Connaught Park that's been a park ... well it wasn't a park ...it was bush and everything else that the kids used to go there and spend ... you know ... times playing and things like that. And of course the hill always has been. We always called it a park even when it wasn't a park. But they had a very nice ski jump on Connaught Hill where they had a I don't know for quite a few years they had a ski jump till one winter there was no snow just like it is now. So they had to give it up, which is quite a loss here. Well we always had a big skating rink, in fact they had a really good hockey team, my eldest son used to play hockey, he was goalkeeper. They had a skating rink outside open ... not like they have a closed one now. It was open and we use to get up at 6 o'clock and go and shovel the snow and clear the ice and we used to go and stand and watch and bounce with our shoes to keep ourselves warm. We used to do that when we were young. We didn't think of it when I was young and my kids were young.*

1971 ~ *Well we had a grocery store for four years and we sold our grocery store to Harold Assman's father. We went into dry goods store and on George Street, which we had it and then we built our own store next to B&B store. I sold to B&B store and we had another building where Carl Strom is which we tore that down and Carl Strom built his own store. Well about five years ago I finally sold the business and sold the store. Madeline loved to travel and had been in different*

places in Europe and New York State and Honolulu. I do love
to travel but I'm just getting too old and I can't do it no
more. After I sold the store I went to live with my daughter
for eight months in Vancouver. Imagine working until you are
81, partly out of desire, but remember there was no pension
attached to her work and the proceeds from the sale of the
business had to maintain her and her daughter for the remainder
of their lives.

1965 ~ As a teenager I was permitted to go with Gammie to
Vancouver on one of her buying trips for the store. I recall feeling
very grown up and important in being allowed to go on this trip. I
think at some level that this type of treatment encouraged a spirit
of independence and confidence that I did not recognize at the
time, but has stood me in good stead over the course of my life. I
was very fortunate to have this influence in my early years.
Imagine my gratitude to know she went through all those things
so that I could have a brighter life, filled with the light from the
candles that she lit ...

After her retirement Madeline kept up a lively correspondence
with several family members. Some of the letters have been saved
and it is possible to see the importance of her extended family in
the following excerpts. Yes, they are difficult to read but I think
they highlight her accomplishments is spite of a limited command
of written English. Once you get the knack of reading her spelling
is begins to read like ... poetry.

October 5, 1967 ~ Dear Daine George and family, ...Got your
leter and Pickchers of your family the sure look nice. George
locks so prowd his baby son on his arms. Wel be 20 years
wen the son be s big es dad. But taym gos fast ... I ws glad
that yowr mother went to Expo see ses see had nice teme see
the country and enjoy her self wery much. I love to go to
Wancower egan for the wenter to ged owey from the snow
and cold. All see leyter wat I do.

1972 ~ Dear George, Daine and family, ... Lynn es getting
marred shes gowing to leve en Prince Rubert hes working.

This Boy es 21 one shel be 20 en October hes working for
Mashen compane. Lynn ses hez got good job. She went ther
to sey the town. He was her for 24 day the desajdet about
the wedeng. Toll and wars glases. The Kegth family lak hem
well. Well be first great grand weding for me. No wonder I
am getting all.

November, 1977 ~ Dear George, Daine and family, ...Nestor
had nice funear big crowd lacts people. Very nice soreves.
Presbetin menester had serweas then Salveshen arme
menester spok about Nestor that he was weal like en White
Rock. The death of her youngest son was a terrible blow and for
several years after she still comments on how sad the occasion
was for her. *I shur meas Nestor. I can belev hes gowan he was*
coming to weset me en couple days estede I wnt to his furer.

November, 1977 ~ Dear George, Daine and family, ... Ar
wenter es her now we got about 2 eah of snow not wery cold
bout slepre ... Ju know that Wallas es Lenda es getting
marred en January 21 first. The having Diner muzek en
Huteal ... The hall es not far from ar house onle about 3
blocks with the Dener and Dance be so we hops we sey ju
her. George I want Danc with Ju ewen I onle 93 stell Jung.
Lest taym I dents 5 year ago Len Knigh weding Leane got 2
years little goel now 5 genereshen. No wonder I am geteng
all.

Although she was getting older she remained a vital part of the
family, tying it together with bonds of love and strength as wife,
mother, grandmother, great-grandmother, and great-great-
grandmother. She sat in the glass enclosed porch of their home
on Seventh Avenue, inviting family and the neighbors in for a
visit. A healthy dose of pragmatism helped overcome many
obstacles as Madeline says in her interview ...

November 25, 1971 ~ Well, we put up lots of hard times but
we were young and we didn't care and we didn't know any
better because that was that.

PRESENT:

On February 9, 2003 I participated, for the first time, in the Prince George IceMAN (but they include woman, too!) Marathon. This is in recognition of the women who invited me to join their team and shared their strength and willingness to have me on this adventure - I do so love an adventure!!

A TRIBUTE TO BREATHLESS

We are five extra-ordinary women
With varying degrees of physical strength
 and ability
And for the record (in order of appearance)

Linda	ski	8 km	cousin and friend of 47 years
Chris	run	10 km	friend of 40 + years
Cherry	skate	5 km	friend of new acquaintance
Kathy	run	5 km	friend of hiking repute
Lynn	swim	800 metres	that's me - good friend of 50 years

Enough to leave you ... **breathless.**

But we did it in 2:46:00 (not a second to spare)
In less time than we imagined
Good enough to place third
That's bronze for this year

Enough to leave you ... **breathless.**

It was the matching headbands
That indicated our willingness
To be publicly united in a common goal
To play in this game, have fun, share time.

Enough to leave you ... *breathless.*

But it was the spirit to compete
The support of comrades
The strength of common understanding
And a desire to be/have it all.

Enough to leave you ...BREATHLESS.

     *   *   *   *   *

FUTURE:

SHARED MOMENT

We met at a conference
strangers.

We left the conference
friends.

Two days of shared
experiences.

What connects two
people/women?

How do we know it is safe to share
our lives, hopes, fears?

Rather than compare the
weather, price of gas, job non-status.

Are you a kindred spirit, found in this
shared moment?

     *   *   *   *   *

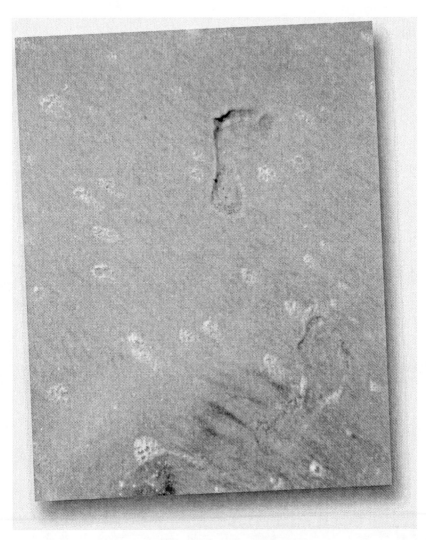

live well, laugh often, love much.
Photo courtesy of Dena Foisy

THERESA HEALY

Preface: about the face you see

I spent my childhood imagining I was someone else, somewhere else. Escaping poverty and abuse with the power of my imagination gave me many gifts other and more than the temporary safety and comfort in the midst of fear and chaos. I have learned never to give up hope that things can and ought to be better than they are. I have never lost a spark from my personal bonfire of believing that we can make change. I have found the power of my mind to create and build with words and images and the courage to risk and trust over and over.

In my past, I have lived many lives: I was taken out of school at 14, ran away from home at 16, lived on the streets and in squats, shared space and Turkish coffee with members of the Bader Meinhoff Gang in Germany, camped on a beach in Belgium and received food from the fisherman's wives. I roamed Europe as a hippy with my first child strapped to my body. I raised my two daughters while trying to support us and my drive for an education   I have worked in factories, nursing homes, hotels, shops, and as a painter's helper. I lived in Mozambique and helped women feed children in a post colonial world that disrupted their traditional child rearing practices. I have been in a union, sat on boards, and marched in protests and staffed picket lines. I have facilitated groups, taught basic research skills and general hell raising. I believe knowledge is power and it belongs to the people. I have received awards and pay cheques. Scattered ramblings and gyspy like transient worker with intellectual skills in my tucker bag as my labour. I try to find space and comfort in the small gaps the big society doesn't consider valuable enough to crush. I try to stand tall even when inside my quivering four year old is rising up determined to be heard. I am determined to do things not only differently but better. My teaching is shaped by students; learning unfolds in the collective acts of the classroom. I refuse to separate workers and earners. I see Goddesses in women in every day.

I never knew a mother's love. The woman who birthed me was raped; I was the result of that violence. I was separated from her at four days of age. In the convent in Southern Ireland it was common for the fallen women to be separated from their children and sent out to work, the children farmed out to adoption, usually to America. If the children were not adopted by the age of four, they were sent back to the mothers. My mother may have loved me, but not that I could tell. Maybe I was always too much of a reminder of something horrific. So.

How do you come to terms with this: that your whole being is nothing more that a violent pain-filled, shame bound memory, constantly picking at the healing scab on someone's else's life?

You do.

I did.

I have learned that mother is a verb not a noun. I have learned to make "mother" in my own image - caring, loving, laughing and always beyond final defeat. I mother my sisters - when they let me. I gather around me women who "mother"; they mother the earth, politics, feminism, and hope. They give birth daily to ideas and promise. They love unconditionally those who walk with them. I gather these women, winnowing through the world of combine harvesters, I walk behind the machine, picking women from the stalks of the left behind, gathering them into a collective of powerful and indefatigable strength. These women build and lift me higher than I can go alone. They hold my hand when I am afraid, when the words and songs at the December 6th memorial bring back terror and remind me it's never over, it's always there, lurking.

And their touch lifts me, they lift me, soaring gently, I hope they are lifted too, reaching for more and better, never satisfied. And that's the answer, Dr. Freud, women want it all, and now and better.

I have wept for the deaths of my comrades and delighted in the joy and strength that women still bring into my life. I live by Mother Jones' Credo: "mourn the dead but fight like hell for the living." I also live by Emma Goldman's "If I can't dance I don't want to be part of your revolution." We have to find joy and the place to dance. We have to believe in ourselves and what we do - it is, after all is said and done, all we have: each other and our actions. And all I have to give you is my word.

Mother as mentor, mentors as mothers

part 1: conception

mother love
mother lode
mother of god
mother fucker
mother of all wars
mother of necessity

I collect mothers the way some people collect stamps or coins, obsessively seeking the perfect one, the one that meets all expert definitions of quality and worth. Is it too self-revealing to admit to choosing partners because of their mothers? Is it just too weird to discard the lover and partner but still hold on to the mother gained?

To replace the mother lost, never known.

Such contradictory notions, how could one frame carry them all, play them all out to the obsessively perfectionist demands of the hungry child, bone tired, soul weary, escaping the clutches of tiny hands that hold tighter than any prison bars to the self.

Feminism gave me a place to understand my mother, to forgive her. But it didn't replace the unrealistic drive to build my own mother.

"My mother made me a lesbian."
"If I give her the material, will she make me one, too?"
Graffiti sprawled on a wall in Kings Cross station, different pens, different handwriting, a cry of blame turned into a funny and shape fitting reduction to normality.

How much power the mother supposedly has, to make one anything.

"Are you going to spend your whole life blaming your mother?
When do you take responsibility for your own life?"

My initial hurt - defensive reaction, I'm not blaming, I insist. I just want people to understand my past, where I came from. Seconds later, sinking in, the power I do have, can take, if I let go of the obsessive need to have her in my life in some fashion, responsible for me in some way. Even if only as reason for my being who I am. I wanted her to be responsible for me and this was the only way.

That question was from David's mother. Not that her success with mothering her own child had been an overwhelmingly successful model of how to do it right. How do you do it right? It's actually set so that you can't. Contradictory and mutually exclusive expectations, pulling women apart, fragmenting their selves and being so that you can't, ever be anything less than inadequate Happy children and clean houses not possible within the same four walls. David still harbouring resentment over his upbringing. What made her work so well as a mother for me?

She was Westmont English, grandfather and father all scions of noble Canadian institutions. I was a dustman's daughter, raised an Irish roman catholic immigrant in a working class British neighbour hood that hated the Irish moiré than any other group on the face of the planet. We blew things up, killed husbands, sons, neighbours. How could they tell, those who harassed me, that I was Irish? The National Front beats up the visible minorities; boover boots and alcohol fuelling their rage. But the generality of the British Populace, ordinary nice people, topped the polls with their hatred of the Irish, but how could they see?

So, how did we fit so well together, me skinny, underfed and uneducated scarecrow and McGill Graduate in Mathematics with perfectly groomed hair, the prototype for Martha Stewart outside of and before a television show and book? I mean, I never even married her son. I was opposed to marriage, a patriarchal construct that oppressed women, a link in the chain of capitalist institutions. Yet she put out photographs of her illegitimate granddaughters and her outlaw daughter regardless of the comments or judgement of other Westmont mothers. Even if we had married, David and I, society's messages about mother and daughter in-laws never getting along - where did that fit in the calm centre that she gave my life? So many women I saw around me liked their mothers-in-law. And if they didn't it, I reckon, it was probably at the same rate of dislike that people carry into any person who lives in their life space.

Her question was blunt - she never did have much tact, went straight to the point. But she genuinely listened to answers, no matter how stumbling or startled the replies. She's probably the reason I am where I am now, sitting at a university desk, pondering how to get a class of what look like ten year olds not to be afraid of me, after I pick up the pieces left behind by the male professor who yells at them for asking questions. I'm writing through demons instead of prepping a lecture (I am two weeks ahead I rationalise - this is good for my soul.)

I want to say, how women can reach across the barriers we are told are impermeable - class and race are real, exist. But. They don't always stand in the way of women. Other imperatives call out and respond. Not that the barriers don't suddenly rise and divide into a path, like the Red Sea for Moses. But how did we, she and I, get to our space.

She still continues to startle me. Her response, when she asked me if I was gay and again, startled by that unexpected directness (you'd think I'd know better after all these years) I didn't even hesitate to do the quick math of "is this a safe place to come out?" but simply blurted "Yes, how did you know?" Her reply was to take my face between her two hands and hold it close. "I know you" she said.

Is this the lesson I have travelled so far to learn? That mother is not a noun but a verb? It is what women do that makes them mothers, not the biological capacity they carry in the uterus. That the face only a mother could love becomes at some fundamental level a choice not a biological necessity? That mothers reach out and touch the heart and soul and spirit and it does not have to be the child they bore that receives the touch. That women can nurture and nourish those who did not spring from their womb? This capacity is what society has stolen and applied only to the birthing process, here this is how you will feel about this child you helped birth. But in fact, the power is much greater and not restricted to only the ones you actually bore yourself?

Is this what adoptive mothers instinctively know, their love for their adopted child is as great as any birth mother's? That my sitting the feet of my favourite poet and matriarch, Jackie, smiling sun in the local sky, is symbolic of the role we can have as women - motherhood as action we can all undertake. Sisterhood is powerful they said in the 60s and I happily embraced the notion of women beside and behind each other, covering their backs, carving new paths through uncharted territory. Motherhood is powerful too, as we birth ourselves and each other. As David's mother birthed the intellectual and academic challenge I became under her tutelage.

And how many other mothers did I adopt, each one birthing another part of my multifaceted, multitalented self. The encouragement of women's eyes and voices in my world, lighting the way forward.

Jacqueline Baldwin, poet extraordinary, I meet her round about, at events about women, and I am always drawn to her side, find myself sitting, literally and figuratively at her feet. Her eyes gaze out at the world, unafraid, always seeking, questioning, almost childlike, wanting to understand. She gathers images, words, events and distils them by some alchemy, long known magic art still carried, into wisdom - powerful words that make you weep, that startle your guts in to awareness, your mind in to recognition -, yes, that's how it is, was, will be. And her gaze, is unwavering, her lips tight as she watches, holding her own voice in to hear others. When she speaks it is with gentleness, forcefulness, power, ruthlessness and compassion at the same moment - see this is the truth, yes it will hurt and no, there is no other way, you can listen and hear and survive and grow.

And how she holds you, when she sees you, "my two favourite lesbians," she says warmly, her smile and her voice warm, no stumble on the lips with the word, no shame, only pride in and of us. She may well say that to every lesbian couple! No matter, her heart is true and real and full.

Mary Lynn Stewart, will she ever realize what she has done in the lives of her students, the difference she made to me. I nearly quit, nearly abandoned the dream of the Ph.D. that I had sacrificed so much for. I had left my children to follow my dream - how not cool was that - leaving my children the way my mother left me. And then to fail, to hate it, feel cheated and betrayed. It was not what I wanted or expected, no challenge, nothing new, just recapitulations and bureaucracy and internal politics- the academic kind, the most viscous Roosevelt said, because the stakes are so small. But she taught me. It's a game, she said, there are rules, you have to be in training, you have to know the players on the other side. I'm your coach. I've watched the other team, I knew them all, the games and tricks, and I'll get you in shape. learn from here, not always easy, post modernism and Foucault, Derrida and Haraway, Riley, All of them, traitors to my hard won feminism, giving me nothing to stand on, or for. Then it clicks. My world turns on its head. I read vociferously, haunting Italian coffee shops, - the price of a latte rent for a street side seat, watching Commercial Drive drift by when I raise my head, lifts from the world of new ideas. And I pass the orals with flying colours, with honours. A different birth canal passed.

Part 2: Birth

Mother love/other love
Finding fragments
That don't, can't, won't, ever fit back together
Patchwork quilt of reasons
Pattern and absence,
Make something bigger
better
warmer

****

You can't see the eyes in the face in the photograph. The woman is looking down and away, a look of anger, at the child in the lap of the woman beside her. They are sisters. The child is hers, but her older sister holds the babe. Does she resent the child, or the loss of her to the sister? Time tells: A later photograph, again, n eyes, she is looking down, away from the camera. In this photo she is laughing, holding a glass of sherry. So rarely I remember her happy, or smiling. Her voice raised more often to swear or in anger than in singing. Rarely, in the same picture with the child. More frequently, wanting absence and distance. Only the father, touching, the only love shown, going too far, not love at all. The mother leaves. The child become mother to the younger ones, father's hands always to be escaped.

******

Part 3: Nursing

Sisters held hands across the streets
then ran.
School berets on at an angle
School satchels carry resistance secrets
Pass through the check points
under watchful sentry gaze
Crossing borders against all odds
delivering

unspoken heroes
French resistance fantasy that
mirrored childhood realm
a safer escape
And grown now,
to learn the truth
That women's lives
forever in occupied territory
Find the resistance movement and join
fight on

So, what the hell difference does it make? A woman births you,
it's as irrelevant as the sperm right?? A donation of the necessary
biological and chemical environment. How much is that donation
worth? The reality is that the mother is more than a womb and a
receptacle into which the sperm passes to find its final resting
place, and out of which the fetus passes to find the world.

Mother emerges later, in the verb, in the act, the verb. Not the
noun. Acquiring a name and distinction through childbirth
doesn't always translate into action, the gap between language
and reality an unbridgeable gap for some women.

So where do motherless women find mothers? We mother
ourselves, creating the reflection and support internally and
seeking it in others to compensate, based on ideals and societal
lies, a better chance of finding mother love than some, trapped
with women who can't love themselves or let alone find mother
love to share with their children. I watch my sisters, one a mother
fiercely protective, all our own mother was not in her eyes, her
strict devotion to mothering. Motherlove unleashed and
unrestricted, almost frightening in its intensity. This is a mother
who would not hesitate to kill if a child were threatened, for
whom desertion and abandonment simply doesn't exist. So
different from my own embattled loving – wanting above all to love
without hurting my daughters as they walk the world. And my
younger 'baby" sister, striving and holding tight to her two big
sisters as surrogates, the only mothering she has ever known, for

our opoposite ends of experience – she will make the best mother
of us all, wedding our two ends in a middle of peace .

Does a dead mother do any more harm than some living mothers?
And dead women, can they mother? Why not? They could. The
women who inspired me, some of them are dead and gone. Emma
Goldman's words "if I can't dance I don't want to be part of your
revolution" an echo that validates fun and pleasure as legitimate
parts of my social justice drive. Mother Jones: "Mourn the Dead
but fight like hell for the living" an anthem that rocks my soul.
Women speaking from beyond the grave, it's worth it, fight on.

And a group of mothers who inspired me - long dead and no
kinship, their courage and how they translated mother love into
political radical action gave me goose bumps, tears rising
somewhere deep inside the first time I heard of them.

You need some "history" the herstory to place these women,
understand the crushing world they faced, Echoes of Campbell's
decimation of the province in 2002 resonating back to the Canada
of the 1930s.

First to understand the power and magnitude of these women to
reach across time, space and generations into my heart. In the
1930's relief was common. Relief was the forerunner of state
support programs Medicare, welfare unemployment insurance, all
of these programs used to be a municipal responsibility, provided
to the "deserving" needy in the community. You qualified if you
"belonged", you were a legitimate resident, if respectable people
could vouch for your industriousness and that your case of need
was not of your own doing and that you had exhausted all other
sources of help. All conditions met, a grudging and usually
material support - not cash, was given as a temporary short term
response.

The Depression, with its rampant surge of unemployment a tidal
wave across the country, began to undermine the ideological
assumptions of relief. Simply too many people were on relief to
support notions of laziness and lack of motivation in the

unemployed. Too many people stood in relief line ups waiting for their rations recognized each other - neighbours, friends, relatives, began to question the systems that suddenly, intruded into their lives. Lack of work seemed to give the state a right to enter the home, to erode dignity and human rights in ways that were so offensive people were traumatized and radicalized.

In Saskatoon, City Council undertook an effort to cut the number and length of council meetings - which were becoming longer and more frequent because council was directly responsible for relief matters. They appointed a City Relief Commission to which the City Relief Officer would report. All relief matters would be referred to, and dealt with, by the city businessmen appointed to the Commission. This would end the endless parade of people appearing before city council demanding attention and services in a public, press covered arena.

In their cost cutting drive the new Relief Commission switched from the City's voucher system. The voucher system allowed recipients to enhance their vouchers for specific goods with their neighborhood grocers. Research had shown that instead of giving the recipients vouchers, providing relief as dry goods and foods would save the city thousands of dollars. Along with this change they introduced a new application system. Which induced an affidavit that spelled out the conditions under which relief would be given. Relief was only a loan repayable on demand, recipients were supposed to take jobs anywhere, any time under the direction of the city, and city inspectors could enter homes any time of day or night. Most importantly, if recipients did not sign the agreement they would be struck of the city's relief lists - in effect, sent to starve.

There were several immediate consequences. In the first place, the autonomy that relief recipients had been able to develop involved relationships with the local grocers was lost. Established local relationships meant that the local grocers could negotiate supplying other goods not allowed by the terms of the voucher system. This informal system benefited both parties, allowing grocers to move other stock and make a small profit off the transaction, and allowed recipients to acquire the things they actually needed but which were not provided by the relief system's vouchers - candles, sewing thread, soap - so little but so necessary. This informal arrangement was termed "abuse" and removing the potential for such abuses was a primary motivator for replacing vouchers with the more easily controlled direct relief. An unexpected outcome was the unlikely alliance of unemployed people and shopkeepers who depended on the City's relief business for their own survival. Both sides were demeaned and diminished by the new system.

In the second instance, people on relief rapidly recognised the inhumanity of the conditions for relief. Ironically, the new system created a space for people to work together - in the line ups, that's where the people normally scattered across the city and carrying out their own individual arrangements in cloaks of shame with their local grocer has not had an opportunity to fully understand what relief was - the close proximity, the forced march into public, exposed the dark underbelly of poverty and relief in daylight.

So people united. They argued the affidavit that was the gateway to relief was wrong. The provision to "sign or else lose relief" amounted to blackmail and the other conditions violated the dignity and rights of people living in a democratic society. 50 families refused to sign. The Relief Commission and nits actions resembled ""Hitlerism" a term used in the 1930s by left wingers aware of the rise of the Nazis in Germany.

From these 50 families, 30 women and their children occupied Saskatoon City Hall. The City hall sit-down strike was designed to draw the attention of City Council and the public to the autocratic and "Nazi" implications of an un-elected body making decisions affecting tax payer funded systems and citizens' lives. The women said the City - through it's relief commission was determined not to feed their children or keep them warm, so they would bring their children to city council chambers where their kids would be at least warm while they starved.

The police immediately surrounded City Hall. The Union of
Unemployed Workers, along with other unions and supporters,
surrounded the police. Local restaurants sent in meals - which
the police let through the cordon. Mattresses and blankets were
rounded up and sent in. The women and kids settled in while the
debate raged outside.

You might argue that taking your children in to what might be a
difficult and dangerous situation an un-motherly thing to do. I
think of those mothers who take their children on those so-called
chains of life to protest abortion. Children too young to think for
themselves paraded with horror stories and parental biases on
cardboard signs around their necks and I know my response -
that's unethical parenting in my mind. Educating and guiding is
one thing, recruiting your children to fight in your own wars is
another. So why does this overtly political act, involving children
not raise the same response in me?

Because I want a mother who takes on the system, who made the
link between motherhood and statehood, who was able to see the
power that the ideology of motherhood held in a time and place
that would have restricted women. It's not about religious beliefs -
that strangulation of thinking exhibited by the fundamentalists
appals me, leaves me breathless at the depth of ignorance and
cruelty a religion can inflict. These mothers remind me of my
ideal of mother, fighter for justice, for home and family, not the
abandoning careless betrayer of my own youth.

Those women won. Their analysis of the relief agreement was
supported by the City Council, who saw votes and public
sympathy lining up on the side of the women.. The Relief
commission was instructed to back off its unrealistic demands.
The system was revised and relief as cash was introduced as a
pilot measure. The test of allowing money as the form of relief
proved that women could manage their budgets and their homes
more economically and effectively than the state could. Children
were able to do their home work because the household budgets
could be managed in way that allowed women to acquire the
things the family needed.

Part 4: Weaning

Held by choice,
committed by reason
loved in tender gentleness
and fierce passion
Justice - no longer blind
But with dancing laughing eyes,
bubbles beneath, between
the ideas of women's worlds

Still seeking, still searching for the mythical. How many women
does it take to construct the ideal - I keep building.
Mothering/mentoring - the coins that shape an economy of
caring. Of women finding places to heal long scarring wounds,
transforming bridges that encourage women to walk into new
worlds with less chance of harm and hurt. A balance of
mutuality, a dance of learning. It goes two ways. Women thank
me, and I pause, struggling to remember what I did. It seemed so
easy and simple, and so little. What little it takes to change the
world. Start now.

YOLANDA COPPOLINO
Rachel Ramble #1

I've been asked to write a biosketch

photo courtesy of Marika Ainley

I'm tempted to first introduce you, Dr. Rachel Carson, but I need to make sure I don't get off on a tangent, because there's a lot to say, and not much time; enough to say that you've inspired me on many levels, and on some levels I can identify with you. I'm always conscious of your legacy in your activism and ground-breaking work on the environment. Your shoes with long imprints so clearly traceable certainly bear no resemblance to mine. Mine so soggy and short, leave only skimpy, muddy-'red' traces!!!! But in terms of your passion and enthusiasm, you are a reminder of my former self; my SELF before retirement, when candles lit around me in a perpetual flame it seemed; candles I'm hoping to re-ignite through this project, spurring me on to continue with others as well. In this regard, with the kind encouragement, creative and continuous support of Si Transken, my mentor for many years, I feel somewhat confident.

Similar to your work experience, Rachel, my work in my teaching days was typically full of passion, enthusiasm and excitement. I taught in the Business Division within the university system, and have since retired. Over most of those years, I lived as a closet feminist. The "f" word was avoided like the plague by many faculty members, both male and female, so my approach had to be sub-rosa but still I think I was able to introduce some of my feminism(s) into the Management courses I taught, albeit obliquely. Also, over time, I was able to gently persuade some of my colleagues to open up the curriculum to include gender issues. Toward the end of my career, we put together a 'Women in Management' course (suggesting that previous management studies excluded the experience of women). It was approved as part of the professional management curriculum, much to the chagrin of some members who considered it almost a sacrilege, a blow to the macho culture that characterizes so many business faculties.

On another level, Rachel, I can identify with you in terms of your relationship with your mother. Similar to you, my mother has been my foundation, and she continues to be the center of my universe. She's a most remarkable individual, an unconditionally devoted mother. I'll talk about her at length again. Also, just as was your experience, my mother has dominated much of my life, in my activities, development of interests, as well as my relationships with friends. I've lived with her all of my life, and the two of us continue to live alone in a house now much too big. And now, also, as was your experience, as she grows less capable, my life revolves around her and her needs. For the most part, as I have to tell my friends (a diminishing number), I'm pretty much under house arrest. Still, I, together with my siblings count ourselves in on a most privileged group. My mother has just celebrated her centenary year and all things considered, she's in fair shape!

I have to keep my fingers crossed however, that her condition will not escalate and worsen quickly, and that circumstances will continue to be such that I'll be able to continue to find some time, scarce as it is, to work on my doctorate. Since 1990 I have been looking at the experiences of women as managers at Eaton's, and at this point, I'm trying to get through rough-drafts of what I'm afraid is becoming an opus-crapus (as my nieces are fond of suggesting to me).

And as is often the case, one door closes and another opens. As I grow older along with my mother, my need to write her-story has become more urgent so that my journal is important in recording our days together. This has led to more introspection and my interest in my Sicilian heritage - language and history. A late bloomer, I suppose, I've become more academically attuned to that culture through the writings of Sicilian authors and of course in addition to my mother's stories of her life in Sicily as the place of her birth. Several years ago, I visited my parents' homes in Sicily (they lived at the opposite ends of the island). It was a home my mother had to leave for Canada some 80 years ago; a home she left against her will, the will of her mother and extended family. Her father was determined she would marry a man of his choice – an Italian in Canada who would be capable of 'caring for her' – Ti fa un pezzo di pani ciu buono – was his theme. Shortly after their arrival, my mother began work in a tailor shop and supported herself and him. A few months later, not being successful in finding a partner that suited him, he began to plan to take her back home, unmarried. However, this time, she would no longer follow the orders of the Zeus, to face the embarrassment of the townspeople back home. She would stay! capable of supporting herself independently she asserted. He returned home alone! In due course, my mother met my father and they were married. However, after only a short period of time, my father passed away. I wish my mother's father could have been present to witness his daughter's (unnamed) feminism, rare in the Sicilian culture, in the 'hag-ocratic' space she independently created for herself and her family, her fortitude, independence, resourcefulness, competency and resiliency.

I try each day to keep a positive attitude; to stay motivated and to avoid becoming 'tentative'. (I use the word 'tentative' to avoid the word 'crazy' in the seclusion of my house-bound life).
Talk to you soon, Yolanda

Dedicated Back and Front to my Mom, my Siblings, my Nieces and Nephews. In this dedication, I introduce you to them as important family-members who are my crutch in different ways and my best friends in every way, and who are an integral part of this story. My special thanks and endless gratitude goes to them.

Unending thanks to my sister, Susan (Assunta) who was my mother's right arm and source of comfort. At age 10, she assumed the role of her English translator in a sometimes unyielding, uncooperative culture. Too, she filled the role of surrogate mother in charge of the three of us, putting together meals for us and my mother when she returned home from work each evening, tired and hungry, often surprising her with 'innovative' cuisinary talents, recipes that were hard to discern! And today, this sister ponders, "What do you tell your grandchildren when they ask, "Nana, what did you do for fun when you were a kid?" - I wish teachers wouldn't give such assignments she cries! With my sister Helen (Elena), both were singled out as outstanding students but they cut their formal education short to help make it possible for my brother and I (as the younger pair) to go to school and to follow professional career paths. We didn't let them down and we are eternally grateful to them.

Helen was most like my Mother, with the same grounded intelligence, natural artistic talents and determination. She was our in-resident house-painter, home-decorator, seamstress, calligrapher. She, like my mother, modelled for me the familiar axiom - my mother's version: "What's a will, it's a Way." But to this day it is stories about her sense of humour and her physical strength in all of her under-5 feet that we re-tell around our kitchen-table when we get together. My mother put her 'in charge' of my 4-year-old brother, Ralph, (Raffaele), a challenge she took seriously. And today we always recall the way she used that diminutive frame of hers to hold him down, kicking and screaming while she forced on his winter boots, tied his scarf around his neck. "Hey, you're choking me"... "Prove it!" she'd say. And with him in tow, off they would go to school together where he sat on his small chair beside her desk until he was enrolled in Grade 1. To this day, the sense of her "might" still enkindles in him a healthy respect. Too, her whimsical ways were a constant source of laughter to all of us including Mom. Often when a verbal discipline was clearly in order, her impromptu reaction would have us all laughing, leaving my Mother as well, laughing helplessly!

Raffaele is the proverbial 'final edition'; the much wanted boy, without whom an Italian family is never complete. Devoted to him, he continues to be my Mother's pride and joy! If ever you want to persuade or convince Mom of something she resists, appoint him as your mediator and ("Thy Will") will be done! Unlike the notion of taking a 'summer vacation' in our world, hard work was no stranger to him either. He fulfilled his professional dream, my mother's dream and our shared dream for him. Much of our coveted psychological support as a family emanates from him, good, forever strong and unwavering. Also, in these days, we can always depend on his physical support, helping with the 'man's work' around the house. While we call him "Ralph" (the anglicized contortion), to my Mom he will always be her "Sonny". To this day a phone call from "Sonny" continues to evoke pleasure and excitement (even though his visits are frequent and routine)! Mom seems to come to life. He completes her day as he did the day he was born. And as the red-carpet treatment is prepared, "My son, my son, and our brother, you make our Candles Burn ever Brighter!"

And to all my Nieces and Nephews, you help make sense of my life. Each one of you and each in your very different ways, inspire me, cheer me, encourage me, help me experience life, give me hope for the future. You're always there, in my heart, on my mind, in my thoughts, in my acts, my interests, my fears, my dreams. You are inextricably intertwined with me. In fact, 'Sei tutti un altro mei stesso!

Rachel Ramble #2

We have to go back some 80 years
The deep heat of the Sicilian sun
Baked deep, with no escape, into your Sicilian bones
It's warm, sand-like gravel stuck in your throat
Choking back the sting of your warm, salty tears
Your Father drags you in tow
All the time telling you he was taking you to Canada for your own
good, for a better life
Your protests were of no avail to this patriarch of patriarchs
You try to BLOCK OUT your Mother's pleas to him to stop, to
return
You force yourself not to look back! Her cries for her only
daughter ringing in your ears
Concetti, la Mamma, non ti vido ciu! (My dearest daughter, I'll
never see you again)!

Two weeks later, a dark dull November day
From the "Vapori America"
You and your father arrive on Ellis Island
And then to Canada, this land called America
Paved with gold!
But the cries never subside:
                Concetti, la Mamma, non ti vido ciu!

        Snow so deep, pavement so hard
        Where was the Sicilian sun, the sand, the salt
        The people so cold, so distant
        Voices so confusing, so jarring, what were they saying?
        Even having NO VOICE was never like this!
        And the cries forever pleading, ringing in your ears:
                Concetti, la Mamma, non ti vido ciu!

But with God's guidance, the sun always rises
And in a few months, it shone brightly!
The pavements on the streets of Hamilton
Made smooth by new friends:

From Racalmuto and Messina
Comare Concetta, Comare Teresa, Comare Caluz, Comare Scadi,
Mamma LaLa, Comare Torre,
Comare Nenni and Za Maria Mazza
Together they brought Papa on the scene
A kind and gentle man
The party was Comare Caluza's idea
And with the game, 'Button, button who's got the button?'
You were to become Papa's cherished Button!
But your pierced heart, still an unhealed wound
The pleas still echoed in your ears:
          Concetti, la Mamma, non ti vido ciu!

And soon, the two of you settled in Toronto
A new house, new friends, new neighbours
Over the next few years, you were a happy couple,
The Canadian sun now so much brighter
Dimmed but never faded out the sound of your Mother's cries
Concetti, la Mamma, non ti vido ciu!

ONCE UPON A TIME THERE WERE TWO ITALIANS
And two Italians happily and busily reared their children
And then there were four of us
Thankfully for you we're sure
The fourth would be the boy that ensured the completion of the
family!

And then the sun went down, the tragedy
Papa's heart failed;
A happy family no longer, you became a single parent
And the words cried out again, more loudly
          Concetti, la Mamma, non ti vido ciu!

But again the Guiding Hand appeared
And together with Eaton's, Mamma Lala (who looked in on us
from time to time)
And the Grossman family who lived upstairs and paid the rent
You carried on
From six in the morning, to eleven at night

The furnace to stoke, the ashes to shake
Our dresses and shirts to starch and clothes to lay out,
The lunches to prepare, the supper to make

And the words continued to drum in the background,
        Concetti, la Mamma, non ti vido ciu!

But you showed us how to live
You grew us, and shaped us
With words so strong,
Work hard, reach high, keep trying, never give up;
A trial show is better than a no-show!

With your guiding mantra, stand proud
You reminded us, "Quanto vale il suo manto, vale il tuo scobba
The sun was out most of the time now!
We grew up together, the four of us,
And you put us through school as best you could

And then three of us married
With good mates, good families and good homes
And now the words like bells rang out,
        Once upon a time, there were two Italians
Before too long, there were 12 'Grandchillun'!!!

But that's not the end of the story
Today, these 12 Grands
Went into the world and multiplied
Remembering that

ONCE UPON A TIME THERE WERE TWO ITALIANS

And brought forth 19 more!!!

And while we know those words continue to tear you:
"Concetti, La Mamma, non ti vido ciu,
There's a happy ending:
As the scriptures say, living to 100 is to be considered a youth
We pray the sun will continue to shine on you!

Rachel Ramble #5

Mom's 100th Birthday Celebration
What does it mean to have an out-of-body experience? I think of
all the months of preparation as an out of mind experience! What
part of the mind: the top of the mind, at the bottom of my mind;
in front of my mind, at the back of my mind? Months and
months of preparation for the celebration and when the day
came, I was in an emotional vacuum. I can hardly remember a
thing about it!

Mindless, mindful
Simple-minded, thoughtful minded
OUT OF MY MIND

Top of my mind, bottom of my mind
Back of my mind, front of my mind
OUT OF MY MIND

Mind-boggled, mind-numbed
Mind-swept, mind-slept
OUT OF MY MIND

Mind-reader, half-a-mind
Mind-bent, mind-blown
OUT OF MY MIND

Sprung-to-mind, mind-begged
Mind-altered, mind-lapsed
OUT OF MY MIND

Mind-candy, mind-gamed
Mind-expanded, mind-shrunk
OUT OF MY MIND

Mind-set, mind-sucked
Never out of my mind
OUT OF MY MIND

Mom's 100th celebration done! my mind at rest
NOT QUITE OUT OF MY MIND!

Rachel Ramble #11

Promises (Racing to Emptiness)

I sit here with all kinds of thoughts raging through my mind.
(Did I mean to say that or did I intend saying 'racing'. Am I really
going mad)?

It was Hannah Wilks who said, "I have to lose my mind to be able
to concentrate." Sometimes I feel that I'm gently sliding into a
peculiar type of madness? Am I mad? I don't know. Maybe.
And Rachel, you come to mind too when you say the discipline of
the writer is to learn to be still and listen to what his (ouch)
subject has to tell him (ouch again). Is working on a thesis really
writing? Is it creative writing? I've never thought of myself as
creative, so why try a thesis. Does this explain why I'm so torn
when I spend time writing to you and I think I ought to be on the
thesis. I want to get it out of the way before I can think about
being 'creative' it seems. Is this the message I keep sending to
myself. And maybe that's what's wrong. To complete this thesis,
I need to FEEL more 'authentic'! Maybe that's the answer.
I wonder whether my doctoral supervisor thinks it's worth trying
to pursue my thesis. I don't know why I care that way except that
he's been very supportive, I respect him very much. But I HAVE
MY DOUBTS that I'm capable of it all. In the back of my mind
I've thought I would write to him except that he's on holidays I
think and he has a sick wife, so does he need to hear from me? Is
this denial?

But what triggered this last spat of anxiety cum 'rage'? Of all
things it was the vase of dead pansies that sits in front of the St.
Francis figure on the hall table. (Poor St. Francis he sure gets
blamed for a lot in my life it seems). Pansies get leggy you know if
you don't pick them regularly and they won't multiply (and we all
want to multiply, don't we, to feel we count). Now, the vase, well,

better wash it and get another bunch of pansies together. Do it
now or you'll forget. And there's the dreaded reminder I placed on
the base of the vase. Why did I have to notice it today? It's a
souvenir from a Stratford trip, 1995. I remember when I took
that trip, remember feeling guilty for taking the day off from the
house and when I could have been spending a little time on my
thesis. And here it is seven years later (if I write it out rather
than use the number 7, it's not as telling and painful). Well,
seven or 7, it's still a long time! Am I really going mad?!

Talk to you again, Yolanda

Rachel Ramble #14

I turn on the radio and Shelagh Rogers is interviewing someone
who teaches play-writing at Guelph U. The interviewee is talking
about how she feels she has to open up her own experiences and
how painful it is. I can relate to that but I haven't written much
about it. I interrupt that conversation and go down to see what
Mom's up to. I sit with her over a coffee-break while she knits her
dish-towels. No cookies or soda crackers today. I try to keep her
mind going so we talk about the brief bit we saw last night on TV
about a woman who had placed her baby out for adoption and
after 45 years was reunited with him. It was a great ending.
Then Mom reminded me that the mother in the show was
reintroduced to the father and they married. Pretty good recall!
She liked that ending, "non come i genti d'oggi", a nicer ending
than most we hear of today.

Here I am; it's morning and I want to talk to you, to tell you what
my day is like and how it seems to shape up more and more as
routine. Up at 8:30 – can't get up earlier, too physically tired. I
take a short walk; make the rounds around the grocery store to
see what's 'interesting' (I can't believe I would ever think a
grocery store interesting). I try to walk fast, but tell myself 'don't
race, just get your heart pumped up'.

When I get home Mom's up; has the coffee set already. So we get breakfast going – peel the kiwi, slice the strawberries and put the raisin bread she likes in the toaster. Ouch, no jam in the fridge, downstairs to check out if there's any in the fridge down there. Ugh, only frozen stuff. Better pick up those bath towels in the dryer while I'm here; don't really need them but...fold and get them out of the way.

Back to breakfast. I'm not racing now either. It's a great day, took our breakfast out to the back. Oh...the moments and movements of my day seem always to be tangled up and connected to my mother. So far she seems happy. I'm afraid to ask her if she wants to go out because I know she will and I know that when she gets back, even if it's just a short trip to the Dominion, she'll be very tired. Settling her in again, putting away the groceries etc, all in all, will take a big chunk of the day. And I really want to try to get some of MY OWN WORK DONE. Usually she wants to go out early because the traffic's heavy in the later afternoon. I know I WILL ASK HER and I know WE WILL GO. She needs the break. But I DO KNOW that yet another day will disintegrate.

Back home, Oops! Before going into the house, I realize it's garbage pick-up tomorrow and they're on strike. Maybe our neighbour will be going to the dump. I really don't want to ask him but he phoned and volunteered to take it. So we're in luck. All I had to do was get the bags ready and get them over to him; (what a blessing)! Oh, have to get to the bank too. I'll be in overdraft if I don't fix up my account so that has to be done TODAY. Pick up films while I'm there; still fretting over Mom's birthday albums, etc. Spent an hour or two yesterday sorting out the myriad of pics. Finally, mustn't forget to call Michael to cut the lawn and make sure I unlock the back gate so he can get in.

It seems so hard to cover all bases these days. And as the saying goes only what is left undone is noticed

Cu fa cento e non fa l'uno
Perde lu cento per il l'uno

Rachel Ramble #15

I'm feeling so guilty about not getting to my thesis; the anxiety is
worse because I know I'm not being productive with any of my
other projects either. I feel so out of touch with myself and most
other things and people. I want to get to my genealogy project
going too to say nothing of my Mom's story and our family story.
Who am I? I think I know most of the time but there's often some
convincing to be done. I'm reminded of the CTV re-run, the
Sopranos and the way they denigrate Italians and those from the
South particularly and the way they try to tear down the culture;
Italy with such a high culture and look what gets communicated.
I hate being identified with the mafia. I should write to them and
protest.

And Scorsese, an Italian too, but denigrating Italians makes good
entertainment and a great money-maker. As one of my nephews
comments, "Can you imagine how entertaining a series would be
about the Irish or Chinese mafia?" His comment prompts the
question:

HOW ITALIAN AM I?
Or "Growing up in a multi-ethnic neighbourhood -
And attending St.Francis School where the teachers were
predominantly Irish and the kids predominantly Italian?
How Italian: Why does it stick in my craw that as kids at St.
Francis School, our teachers, Miss Jennings, Mr. O'Hara,
Miss Hennessey, etc. plugged us into St. Patrick's Day
concerts "Oh Danny Boy" and "When Irish Eyes are Smiling",
year after year? Where were Santa Lucia and O Solo Mio?
How Italian: And in Grade 4 why did I admire Miss Kelsey so
much?
How Italian: Why did they call me YolAnda and not YolOnda?
How did it make me feel?
How Italian: Why do I spell my name with a "Y" instead of the
Italian "i lunga, J"?
How Italian: Why was 'Raffaele' foreign to the teachers? "Well,
we'll just call him "Joe". How does it make you feel?
How Italian: What's worse, why was I ashamed at school that
our mother spoke broken English?

How Italian: Having her centenary party at the Old Mill, does that mean "you've made it in the world of the mangiachech", asks a nephew?!
How Italian: How come it seemed to my nephew that there were so many non-Italian friends at the party?
How Italian: So many non-Italians? Maybe it looked like that because none of our nieces and nephews married Italians? And why didn't they marry partners of Italian extraction? Who will keep the flame burning? How does that make any of us feel?
How Italian: Why did we move to the Beach with its Anglo tennis courts, white shorts and sneakers - away from Manning Avenue, our Italian neighbourhood, baseball on the streets, and Mr. Belli's Saturday night chirchiachi, serenading us as he strolled home from the bar and as his kids scurried into the house closing the door behind them, horribly embarrassed? (Do roosters crow in Italian only? Is this the way of Italian men only?)
How Italian: Yet we kept our Italian friends close to us over the many years, all of us, in spite of our new-found non-Italian connections? How do we explain this?
How Italian: Why did I yearn for more Italian symbols at the party and why didn't I do something about it?
How Italian: How did I become so ambivalent about my cultural roots anyway?
How Italian: Why was I surprised to find a book entitled, "Beginner's Sicilian. Isn't the Sicilian dialect a taboo, and isn't "Sicilianese" to be cleansed out of the Italian culture?
How Italian: Why does it bug me so much when I'm introduced for the first time with the inevitable comment, "Your husband must be Italian" (assumption: grey eyes are not "Italian", as a female you must be married and you must have taken your husband's name)?
How Italian: Why do I yearn to go back to Manning and College?
How Italian: Why am I so hounded by these questions?

Vado, Rachele, ti vido al ritorno, Jolanda

Rachel Ramble #18

The Promises/Races to Emptiness

I think of Eric Maisel who talks about the hushing principle:
stopping your mind from operating on **autoscan**, rushing from
one useless/meaningless/something important (not too often)
thing to do before I can settle down.

I AM on autoscan for sure right now! How do you stop it? I made
promises to myself yesterday, promises that I would be more
productive. I made these promises when I was too tired to do
anything else. It's a little like deciding to go on a diet after you've
had a full meal. I'm still racing around on AUTOSCAN! How to
deal with it? I used to make out 'to-do' lists but that doesn't work
too well when you don't control much of your day and your life is
full of minutia, inconsequential at that. I just move from one
more thing and then another and one detail completed surfaces
yet another. I sometimes feel like my hand/my head/my entire
body is bound by a live elecrical-wire. Reminds me of when I was
a kid and my brother and I cried as we watched my mother
strangle a chicken, wringing its neck. It would flail wildly,
struggling so frantically for survival. I can't help feeling like that
chicken, struggling for the survival of my own creative life!

And all the time I'm afraid of becoming the person who's doing
the doing, and doing and doing – nothing! Empty-headed, tired
and forever having a ton of details to attend to. I look around me
and find bright women like my friend, Maria, with a husband who
has become disdainful and even contemptuous of her because
she has 'neglected her intellectual development' over the years in
spite of a life full of caring for four kids and for him, a husband.
How depressing! Is it all a zero-sum game after all for women?

Again, I'm feeling guilty. The day is whizzing by and I'm still here
writing to you. On the other hand Eric Maisel talks about the
need for artists to paint, actors to act and writers to write so at
least I'm writing today. Not for long though; I have to get down
and start up lunch. Mom will be getting hungry and so am I.

How things have changed; Mom who waited for no one, now waits for me to initiate lunch.

And so my life on Autoscan continues. It's really everywoman's life.
I think this piece, its incoherence, IS appropriately called "racing to emptiness"

Al presto, Ciao bella, Jolanda
Pazienza e sapienza! (Patience brings knowledge (or so they say)

Rachel Ramble #22

I've been looking for a way to settle down

Over the past few days , there seems to be no reprieve to my autoscanning life. I'm so much dependent on Mom's state, health, feelings and mood. Although she's not a moody person, she's irritable when she doesn't feel well, and no wonder. The past few days, since Sunday, she's been feeling terrible. No energy, head-aches and she looks pale and drawn. Makes me wonder if that's what 'slipping away' looks like, very unnerving and frightening. I keep wondering what's going on in her head at this point as things swirl around in mine. She doesn't talk about death too much. I know I ought to record these days with her but I just can't bear it, to deal with writing it all out. So like Scarlett, I leave it for tomorrow.

Rachel Ramble #27

What a mind!

It's like being on a roller-coaster. This morning, thank Goodness, Mom's much brighter and quite alert.   She asks about when the hockey season will start. She likes hockey and looks forward to watching the Maple Leafs on TV. She particularly likes Sundin because he scores a lot of goals but most of all she likes Ty Domi. She likes his feistiness! Calls him Pie-Dough: to her ear, "TY" sounds like "Pie" and to her, his round face is pie-like. Hence we always share a chuckle over PIE-DOUGH.

Sometimes these 'alert' days get a little rocky and today is one of those days. I began the day thinking as soon as I attend to the Mountain Ash (it looks like the caterpillars are at it) and arrange the flower pots I promised myself I would organize my room, sort out my projects. I bought four in-trays yesterday for that purpose. (Interesting that I call them all "in-trays" – an omen? that there won't be anything going "out", but I have to try not to be negative). This is all in the name of DOING MY OWN WORK, getting back to my thesis and a semblance of order in an effort to clear my mind at a time when I've come to think I'll never ever have a clear thought again. Mom came down feeling pretty well. While much slower now, her determination is clear, a determination that sometimes gets in our way so much so that we're like frick and frack. For example, after fixing the plants and as I make my way upstairs to start MY WORK, she called me down. I found her on the porch re-arranging all of the same plants, undoing what I had just completed, doing it her way and, she asks if I like the arrangement? Maddening, but thankful that she's still interested and well enough to do it.

Once back upstairs I unwrap my thesis folders (brittle with age and dormancy) again to DO MY OWN WORK! That phrase has a special resonance for me. As a young secretary, the boss kept me so busy I complained that I had no time to DO MY OWN WORK such as fixing up manuals for MY use to help me keep him straight. His response, "Well, whose work is a secretary supposed to do?" What he meant was that if I had responsibilities that did not emanate from him directly and focus directly on his needs I ought not consider it work, not real work and certainly not important work. Like a wife, I think this resonates for most women, a kind of a flesh-eating disease.

And now decades later, have I come full circle? But while looking after the house CONSUMES ME, my relationship with my Mom, a daughter's love for her mother and a mother's unconditional love for her children, defies the relations that patriarchy demands of us, of her, of me. This 'hag-ocrat's' adjustment to retirement and entry into the R E A L, 'real world', is not easy!

Rachel Ramble #29

'Women's work, Men's work, Ever Thus!

In putting the car back in the garage today, I'm reminded of the hole in its ceiling. We need a handy-man. A neighbour leads me to Louis who quotes $185 just to repair a hole about 12"x 14". He tells me it's a two-hour job, and he lives up the road from us. I guess handy-men come in handy at some point but sometimes you have to wonder how 'handy' is defined when I probably could do the job myself if I put my 'handy-head' to it. Some $200 is way over my budget for such a small job! Makes me think about how our work as women is undervalued and how we, as women, are complicit in this under-valuation of it. I know, Rachel, you encountered tastes of it in no small amounts in your relations with the government as a woman on a man's turf. My thoughts today though are about my sister, Helen. An excellent seamstress, she was fretting about charging for a pair of drapes she was putting together for an acquaintance. Sewing drapes is complicated and requires skills that take many years of training and experience to perfect. There's a lot of material to handle, patterns to match, awkward measurements to take, hooks to place, plackets to measure and sew, linings to cut and fit, etc. It took her more than two full days. And yet she angsts over charging $100 for the entire job! While I could bumble through plastering up the hole in the garage I know there is no way I could put those drapes together, NOR COULD HE!

Rachel Ramble #30

What about this candle of life? If only women counted...for themselves, as women!

What about the time when this wick is all spent (wick as in witch)?
I put my head back on a chair. Do I leave a mark?
Will I leave a mark?
On whom? What will it be? and Why do I care?
What does it matter?
As a woman, a single woman at that, will anybody care?

And what is it about marriage that silences us?
And what about my married sisters? What about them and their mark?
Who will know about them and their lives?
As married women, wives and mothers
Who will even observe their work, much less celebrate it?

After so many years, it's only now as husbands die, work patterns change
And their overall circumstances change that I am learning about the reality of their lives
        their real lived experiences?
Who are they as individuals, separate beings, Independent Selves?

If only women counted...for themselves, as women!

Ciao per oro, Rachella, Jolanda

Rachel Ramble #39

My Projects

Most of my projects are interrelated and I look forward to that aspect of them - so much more interesting and fun.

Project #1: Finish my doctoral thesis – what's to say about that that could be original?

Project #2: The 'This Ain't' book, my piece to be written. So much of what I have to say here is interconnected with other projects and other parts of my life so it's a very exciting project.

Project #3: Family genealogy: Mom's story, working in my own memoirs, siblings, nieces and nephews

Project #4: Organize old photos – as part of project #3

Project #5: Mom's birthday albums for my nieces and nephews; correspondence with friends re her celebration; pictures to be developed, etc.

Project #6: Collection of Mom's proverbs and related stories

Project #7: Read a book – one a month is probably realistic 'til I complete my thesis

Project #8: Pull Mom's recipes together. This is a major work as they're mostly all in her head.

Project #9: Yippee: Plan a trip to SICILY to the home of my parents!

Project #10: Look at my finances. This task always puts me in a bad mood and is always at the bottom of my pile.

The list is sometimes overwhelming but brings to mind my mother's philosophy:

Chi vogli assai, nenti ha! And
Si mi rieschi si chiama Nicola e si no, Nicola com era!

Loose translation: Wanting too much may result in gaining little but you must have
a plan. If it's successful, Nicola will be transformed. If not she'll remain Nicola as was!
OR, Reach for the sky. After all, what's a heaven for?

Nothing ventured, nothing gained!

Ti scrivo, cara Rachel, al ritorno! Jolanda

Rachel Ramble #43

Feeling like I'm nowhere

Have felt this way for weeks, maybe months, but since Mom's attack (I hate that word with a vengeance) I just don't know what I'm about. It was hard enough to understand that before so you can imagine how it feels when you have to watch the person who is virtually the centre of your universe suffer so much. Not even do I imagine limbo or purgatory to feel like this, and that's a pretty desolate thought.

I look around me these days, these nights, these mornings, these evenings, and I'm really having trouble making sense of anything. Nothing is important to me, yet every single detail is taking on extraordinary significance – everyone of Mom's movements, bits of conversation, every lament, every twist of her body, every pull on her blanket, push on her pillow, all tell me about this wonderful, extraordinary, undervalued woman, this Mother. How did she play the different roles we like to talk about as women? How does feminist theory explain someone like her? To me and to all of us I'm sure, our Mother was never anyone/anything else but a mother, a mom, Mamma! Never thought of her in any other way, yet she was a daughter, a lover, a wife, a widow, a breadwinner, a seamstress, a grandmother, a sister, a niece, an aunt.

At 100, so close to the end of her life, it's – an inevitable reality that we all as a family have to face. (This is the first time I've put it into words. Damn, damn, how I wish it were another one of my many misconstruals and misunderstandings about life and what we're doing here)! I know **death** is a certainty and I can **live** with this irony. Drawing a hard-life card, living a self-less life, I can understand also, but to have to endure a painful old age, how is that justified? I wish I had a deeper faith right now. I need to hear the comforting voice of a 'Mother'. Where in the 'Mother

Church' is that mother? All I can see right now is the irony of it
all!

Rachel Ramble #44

Again, it's been a really disjointed, distracting morning

It started out so well. Went for a walk, started to formulate in my
head a short segment of my Mom's story. I found her up when I
came home, looking and feeling well, a nice change! We sat down
for breakfast, and she said her usual grace, the short version
when there's just the two of us: "Saluti, God Bless my family, God
bless the table." I thought about the way little Paul, my nephew,
always laughs and asks, "Why does Bisnonna want God to bless
the table?" How much we'll all miss you, Mom! In a few minutes,
she feels sick again, deep chest pains. Again, my heart sinks. I
give her a nitro pill. And so another morning vanishes, not
wasted, just not productive. Worrying about her takes a lot out of
me and I really can't concentrate when she's like that. Yet, would
I trade this symbiotic relationship – Never!

The little piece of her story I wanted to get down on paper was so
clear at one point. Fortunately, it's not all gone, I was able to
recapture some of it:

Rachel Ramble #49

The year 1934, Papa's Prognosis

Dr.Sansone: Con lavoro a la fattoria, non vedi la stagioni!
Deve riposare a letto! If you continue to work, with your heart,
you'll be dead by the end of this summer! Ti fasso la carta per il
governo per 'welfare'!

It was 1934, in the thick of the Depression and Mom, you well
knew what it meant when you heard the ominous words, "il

governo and welfare" strung together. The dreaded government 'relief' fund would step in to feed your family - the food-baskets that so many of the neighbours lined up for every week that you had avoided. Like the pogey, you always prayed that would never be part of our lives. You looked at Papa and in his eyes you could see his heart sink as well. And as his eyes welled up with tears, he said, "Concetti, ti racomando, prima principale, no fa sapere i mei parente in Sicilia (don't let his family know, don't bring disgrace to them).

In spite of the Depression in its early years, things had been going well for us. Papa had a job in the cigar factory, made a labourer's wage but it paid ok. And when you found you were pregnant again, number 4 (and this time it would be hopefully, the long-awaited boy), you knew the flat on Wolsely Street was too small. So you took the plunge and looked for a house to buy. The one you found on Manning Avenue was perfect, modest, but perfect mostly because it was brand new. 'New' that was the operative word for you. You didn't want to deal with 'unexpected stuff', the usual stuff people leave behind when they're looking forward to better things. You didn't want to have to do their cleanup; you've always been so proud, so smart. The mortgage was hefty but you were such a good manager. It was just a 6-rom house but you made it big enough to hold the six of us, and rented a flat upstairs. With Papa's pay and the $14 a month rent, you managed to meet the mortgage payments, principal plus interest (not always a common accomplishment) and on time every month (also not common in those days). And as you sewed most of our clothes, we were dressed better than most (in those days), fed us well and kept us out of debt.

And now this! 'Government Relief', the ugliest words for you in the English language. How much you hated the very thought of it, of being unable to look after yourself, "Ho besogni aiuto per sostenire la mia famigilia?! No! No!" But life went on. Papa stayed home. He tried to get used to it, to resting, but he knew there was no getting used to being on 'relief'. That pain did not go away. And so one day, you told him you were going to Eaton's – the kids need new socks you said. And there in the Eaton's

Annex, you were fortunate enough to be waited on by a kind
'salesgirl' who treated you with respect despite your Italian accent
(Italians were not the most welcomed of immigrants). You bought
your socks. Sensing a kind spirit you made the salesperson
understand that you needed a job, that you could sew and you
could tailor. She pointed in the direction of the red building.
"Right across the street, next to the Salvation Army building, go
in there. I'm sure somebody will help you."

And Eaton's tailoring factory did hire you, almost on the spot.
The man operating the cage-elevator said, "Ok, lady, on the third
floor and ask for Mr. Jamieson." There, just as he said, you were
relieved because you **were** greeted by Mr. Jamieson – no red tape.
You were successful in making him understand: your brother in
Italy had taught you the tailoring trade and you were good at it
AND you needed a job!" "Ok, come back tomorrow (Saturday) and
we'll see what you can do and if we can use you." Evidently he
liked your work and he told you, "Come back on Monday and you
can start work." You were elated though you worried about the
way Papa would take it. As you suspected, he was devastated: "E
gli toi parenti?" What are they in Racalumuto going to say when
they hear Gabriele Coppolino cannot work, "non poi soportari la
sua famiglia. Shame!! Nevertheless, it made good sense to you,
your prideful but practical self! And if you worked hard, proved
yourself as a finisher, 12 stitches to the inch on men's over-sized
coats, Eaton's would guarantee you a wage of $12.50 plus
whatever you earned on piecework, every 5 ½ day week. So,
which was worse? The humiliation in having to be on 'Relief' and
to rely on the 'Governo' for handouts to pay your bills and feed
your family, or working to support your family yourself,
independent of everyone. And you persuaded Papa with, "Senti,
non e per sempre" - just until you get on your feet, strong enough
to go back to work.

But that 'until' never came!
Papa's heart finally gave up!
February 4, 1936
And a new stage in your life was about to begin!

Mom, a widow, 34 years old, married 12 years, migrated from Sicily, Italy 13 years previously; "English, the spoken word and comprehension almost nil (Papa had done most of the talking that was necessary). But the story just begins.

You were now a single parent - no, not a 'single parent' in those days. Rather you were a WIDOW and we were not 'your children', we were ORPHANS.

And the prospect of that much dreaded Government, 'Il Governo', rears its ugly head again. Once a month they checked up on you and on us; to make sure you were feeding us properly; spending the government 'Allowance' properly and I guess, that there were no live-ins helping you out.

But this was not for long. The government really didn't know you. You worked day and night, took work home, threaded your needles at night to get ahead for the next day's piece-work, rented your rooms, sewed our clothes and put together enough income to **SEND HER AWAY! Please don't send that Government Lady (the social-worker) to my house again! I can look after my own children!**

Io sola sopporto i mei figli e Io sola comando sopre la mia famiglia!!

Tanti cari saluti, Rachella, Jolanda!

Rachel Ramble #51

I'm really at odds today.

Not that I've been much on 'evens' most other days lately, but today I feel like a gyroscope. Twirling around, flitting up, flitting down, flitting every which way – twirling, twirling, my head keeps spinning. Is this what retired spinsters are all about - no beginning and no possible end in sight? What's my purpose anyway? What am I doing here? To accomplish what - only to hear the loud reply, "Zero, that's what!"

Accomplish – zero!
I think that's what I should call myself.
Yes, my name is "Accomplish Zero"
Now make sure you pronounce it right
It's got to have exactly the right amount of bite
So it will hurt
That is, you have to say,
You're Italian after all,
ZERRO, rhyme it with 'marrow'

And make sure you roll the rrr's
You have to feel it in your bones
That way it really hits home!

Yes, that's right
My full name is "Accomplish Zero"
Looks great on my Bio, eh?

Am I being too negative?
Too hard on myself?
I don't think so,
If I were I'd crawl out of this man-hole.
Well, maybe not; after all it IS a man-hole isn't it?
And my parents were Italian immigrants weren't they?
So what's this woman – daughter, spinster, aunt - doing down
there, he asks?
Diggin' in her own woman-hole, of course.

And now that that's said and DONE,
I feel better,
I'm DONE
I found my purpose

And my name IS
Accomplish Zero

Rachel Ramble #53

I've been asked to write a biographical sketch.

I've been putting it off. You know why! It means I have to 'look at myself', and these days, you know by now, I'm not impressed with myself. But I'm sitting here in front of Eleanor Roosevelt's stern warning: "You must do the thing that you think you cannot do!" And this applies to the task that requires the bio-sketch as well as the work on my thesis.

I ask myself often why this thesis is so difficult for me. And I always come to the same answer. I can't seem to get motivated, and why can't I get motivated? Have I become that person who is driven only by the promise of some extrinsic – a job, a promotion? I've never been that person. I entered into the PhD because it is something I've always wanted to do but I involved myself so much in my teaching that I made no time for it. On the other hand, as the saying goes, you make the time for what you want to do so on that front I failed. On the third hand though, I WAS filling my time with something that I was passionate about. I started teaching relatively late in life within the high-school system. My motive in retrospect was pretty altruistic. I wanted to help teenagers to become aware of the sexism that is part of our culture in an environment that was hostile to any kind of 'feminist' thinking. I was there for only a few years when I was offered a position within the university system, and I leaped at the opportunity, thinking there I could develop my own courses and incorporate in them some feminist principles. I was aware that feminism was still the "F" word but I thought I would have more freedom at this level, particularly in teaching management courses. On one level, I was successful but my approach to feminism, nevertheless, had to be anything but overt.

Over the years, I was appointed Chair of the department. While I thought I would have more freedom in that position to spread the 'word', I found it was a tough hoe particularly as the only female Chair in the Business Division. As a female, negotiating for budgets for example to get the gender courses I wanted was not

going to cut it. After a few harrowing experiences, I found I was
more effective by encouraging faculty, and there were a couple -
only a couple - who were committed to feminism who were a great
help.

Overall, this stage in my career was an isolating experience, but
gratifying in some ways. I think the most rewarding was in
developing and getting approval for a "Women in Management"
course by our department and through Academic Council. This
course survived over several years in the midst of the
androcentric worldview of management faculty who denied the
existence of sexism, thought business/ management was gender-
neutral, and referred to such a course as 'fluff'. Most interesting
was the notion that some of the male faculty members offered to
teach the gender course and were astounded to learn they would
have to take some fairly extensive professional development to
bring themselves up to a minimum level of competency. They
never did teach it. The course was successful and 'evolved' well.
Over time, however, feminist faculty left, and guess what, the
course became 'Managing Diversity". Well, there are covers and
there are covers!

Rachel Ramblings #55

On Being an Aunt

You didn't have sisters, Rachel.

But you did have nieces and nephews so I think you are able to
relate to my current frame of mind at least on some level. I've
always thought how irrationally our relationships change with
our sisters, nieces (and other loved one – parents, etc.) once as
women we marry. It's as though our relationship to the emotion
of 'love' for one another, once so loving, so unconditional, so open,
automatically, it seems, once married, become transformed,
bounded and finite. No longer, it seems, can it be sustained. No
longer shared in the same way, sister-to-sister, married sister to

single sister, married niece to single aunt. No longer is there
space once a husband enters into the relationship it seems.

I want to talk about this pain we can create in our love
relationships with family members within the context of the
traditions and demands of the 'holy sacrament of marriage' in our
patriarchal world. These thoughts were re-triggered this morning
when I heard a poem read on the radio about a niece whose
favourite aunt, a single person, was dying of cancer. The heart-
wrenching ache it caused her as she went over her happy years,
growing up with this aunt, the games they played, the books they
read together, the stories and secrets they shared. Now how so
fortunate she was able to nurture this aunt through the period of
her cancer, shared her love and pain, and helped comfort her as
she was coming to the close of her life.

As you know, I'm a never-married woman; a single person. I have
a niece, one of many, all of whom are very dear to me. This one
became exceptionally close. For many years we were on the same
faculty. Some people said we were joined at the hip. Now
married and in the midst of an emotional upheaval by the
sadness of a marital separation, the sorrow and anxiety I feel for
her, hidden and forced into silence by tradition, betrays the
anguish of the emotional separation, emotions I feel so
intertwined with hers.

How her experience in an unhappy marriage has ripped at my
heart, every day, every night, and how silence over time only
makes it worse – time that mythical healer. My sadness grows
and often so suddenly, its pangs of pain burst out of nowhere it
seems. Oh, the sweetness she's always brought into my life - as a
child, the dandelions she picked in a bouquet for me, the games
we played together, the stories we made up as the sandman filled
her eyes; as she grew up, the dreams, wants, expectations and
fears she shared with me.

Rachel Ramble #65

Disappointments, disillusionments and the continuums
approaching these spaces
My niece, do you remember...?

You followed me into the classroom and we shared offices as well
as many of the same students. We shared stories about almost
anything and everything.

I want to talk to her, to remind her. Do you remember those
laughs we had together? Do you remember telling our stories
about how the students managed to outfox us by allowing them
to set their own due-dates on assignments (in the name of
feminists' flexibility), only to leave us both holding the bag – a
ton-full of papers to mark on a long weekend while they lined up
on the ski slopes. And the happiness we shared when our
students did well, asked good questions, wrote good papers.

How so like-minded we were! As some observers were fond of
saying, "You two are joined at the hip AND at your head." Do you
remember?

And do you remember the tensions we felt (mostly needless) in
course evaluation week, and when due dates piled up on us. But
no matter what, you could always make me laugh. Remember
how you would remind me that some of the barnyard language,
the double-entendres in comments by some academics, mostly
men, were a waste of their time because, "Auntie Yo, that one was
lost on you, wasn't it!" And we'd make fun of it all, of them, of
me, of ourselves. They were kind, healthy laughs, never
malicious, just funny. You always made me laugh even when I
was mad or sad, because you're so funny.

Yes, for so many years, all of your life in fact, you just plain made
me laugh!

And then when you married to the 'love of your life', we were all
so happy for you!

Rachel Ramble #66

The Code of Silence, again!

But after a while things changed for my niece. She was unable to share her life with me as before. Our heart-to-heart talks became fewer and fewer. Slowly and little by little occasions of small talk, big talk, fun talk that touched our funny-bones, sad talk that touched our sad-bones became scarcer and scarcer.

And now, that the love of her life is out of her life, she feels even more so that she cannot share the disappointment and the disillusionment. Large signs spelling out the Code of Silence for married couples hang high overhead: 'Cover up'! 'Please Do Not Expose!" 'Keep in a Hidden Place'!! Away from those who love you most! 'Private, married couples' problems are no one else's business. All taboos. I watch her go about daily life, silently now, methodically, never giving in, never letting on the pain, pretending cheer. You are trying to be a type of strong, my dear niece, that needn't be...

My dear niece, these thoughts are for you:

You must know this single aunt's candle WILL always glow for you
It will always burn ashes of love for you

Keep in mind, the power of Love IS infinite
Loving relationships ARE a renewable resource, and
No patriarchal social construct CAN change that!

Ciao bella nipote! Zia Yolanda

Rachel Ramble #68

Our "Italian HIJABS, Our SELVES

Again, I'm all twisted out of shape - such a flow of different emotions, from anxious disquietude, to anger and disillusionment. I'm so sensitized to my identity/MIS-IDENTITY and the fact that I wouldn't allow myself to face it. Now here I am, feeling the way I should have 40 years ago.

I feel our family is 'every Italo-Canadian' family, numbed, leading the path bloodied with the patriarchy of our fathers toward its own extinction. Growing up at a time when it was made clear to our parents as Italian immigrants and as their children, we were the 'natural underclass', unwelcomed and inferior, we coped by covering up our true selves. Anxious to swim in the mainstream, we hid the 'shame' of our bloodstream in our 'Hijabs'. The memories of the painstaking efforts we made to fit into and to become what the state wanted our parents to be: "English-style immigrants", to become accepted into a culture we had little idea of except that we were continually reminded, and of so amply made aware, so convinced that to be Anglo was indeed superior, served to fill us with a deep sense of self-loathing and self-disgust for who we were, how we looked and how we behaved. And little did we realize the nature of the 'help' to change that we were given. The xenophobia that surrounded us, our environment, school, teachers, government, all, some unwittingly, ensured that our self-loathing was perpetuated within ourselves, would keep us In Our 'Hijabs', and KEEP US IN OUR PLACE. Without a voice from our immigrant parents, powerless and uncertain, to shout, to remind us: "Remember you are Italo-Canadians, be proud."

Today, in even the most mundane of acts and experiences, I feel so deeply the pains of our self-sabotage:

We ALL hated our Names. Helped by our Irish teachers, in their limited capacity to strain their Irish ear. For example, Fortunatina became Tina, Anna became Anne, Assunta became Susan, Helen

- Elena and Angelina - Angela. Raffaele, well, he became "just Joe."

We hated our Looks too. Why wouldn't our black, tempestuous hair lie flat like so many of our non-Italian friends? Why did my sisters want to show me off – a trophy – so proud because their little sister's eyes were grey and not brown and her hair was brown, not black. Why was it that none of our Italian Moms were tall, slim and aquiline like those in our story-books and movies?

And worse, we Pretended To Hate everything and anything Italian from 'pasta cu lu sugo' (spaghetti and tomato sauce), to music, from Frankie Lane to Frank Sinatra, to Italian ballads, "Non ti scordar di me" to "La vesta bianca" and "Santa Lucia, bacchetta mia."

While we pretended some hates, most regretful in our behaviour was our disinterest in learning to speak our mother's native tongue. Most despicable though was the resentment some of us felt toward our mother: Why wasn't she more like some of the parents of our 'Canadian' friends', take a joke, understand or share a joke, play a game with us? Share a book? And why did she have to work ALL the time? Why was she always in a hurry? Why did she seem so agitated all the time?

Our HIJAB was most poignant and a continued source of self-loathing for me today in the way I HID her from our English-speaking friends; this, the most caring, beautiful, intelligent human being. I was ashamed of her, not of her appearance which was beyond reproach, but her broken English. I feared people would not understand her – afraid that friends and teachers would make fun of her. She would be embarrassed. Today, my shame asks the question, "Whose embarrassment was I fearing?"

But it was this English-illiterate woman who was so intelligent as to understand the 'Selfish Gene' so well as to choose to remain single after our father died. Proposals of re-marriage in exchange for a promise of an easier life in a hostile culture and an economy that was calibrated in such a way as to make it impossible for a woman to earn enough money to support four growing children were of little interest to her. With her strong sense of self and independence, she knew she could/would/and did do better herself, on her own. And in addition, this semi-literate mother understood the value of education so well as to pass it on to her children, to make sure they were well enough educated to avoid the sweat-shops that were her experience, an accomplishment that many of our peers at the time, including those who had fathers, could not achieve.

And there is a happy ending:
In the candles that burn in the eyes of my Nieces and Nephews:
Nowhere do I see the scars left by the HIJABS that were ours
Nowhere do I see the expectation of privilege in the eyes of my nephews!
And in so many ways I see in all of them
My mother's values, resilience, fortitude, honesty, diligence and creative essence

In my mother's proverb, there is hope after all: Male tempo, bon tempo, non dura sempre un tempo!

Ciao bella for now, Jolanda

Rachel Rambling #90

She's/we/re so agitated today! My mood so down!

I sit here today and I'm full of all kinds of different emotions and tensions. I want to cry but I know it won't help. I've done that before, many times thinking the release would help. It does not, and today I WILL NOT GIVE IN!!

It's 1:30 pm, Tuesday, and Mom is still in bed. She's had a terrible morning! More and more this is the case. This morning it wasn't just her bones that bothered her but a combination of pains, aches all over her body, from her chest, shortness of

breath, arms, legs, every limb aches. I listen to her cries. She's
mentally alert. She tells me "I don't want this life, I want to do
the things I can't do anymore, I want to die". And so it goes.
She's/we're so agitated today!

I try to concentrate on something – just anything. Make some
chicken soup? Work on my part of Si's book? Read a book?
Read my e-mails? Write some e-m messages to the dozens of
people I owe? Get back to my thesis...make some lunch...wash
some clothes? Pray! Call my brother, sisters? Nothing seems to
work. Everything's at odds. Nothing makes sense! And she's so
discouraged!
She's/we're so agitated today!

I move closer to her bed now; sit in a chair in the corner of her
room; I wait, I listen for her every moan, every move, every breath
as she moves around the bed, restless. I help lift her, turn her,
raise her head, hold her hand – so cold! Her intelligent eyes, her
expression once so vibrant, interested and interesting, buried now
in her helpless, broken frame.
She's/we're so agitated today!

I notice how light she has become, like a feather now, her arms,
hands, every part of her so fragile. Mom, what happened to the
reassuring grip of your hands you so often put in mine, so
comforting, so firm? And your arms so strong, you hugged me so
tight? They were so lithe and at the same time so powerful and
reassuring. Remember when the Grands were growing up, they
couldn't get over your muscles, your strength. You would
challenge them with the "rompa me". They could never bring you
down!
She's/we're so agitated today!

Sometimes on mornings like these she'll get up and take a short
walk around from one room to another. Today she wants some
help. She forces herself to stand up but can't. So I just tuck her
back into bed. She dozes off for another few minutes. I watch.
Complexion so sallow! Wasn't it just yesterday, her high

cheekbones so full and rosy, so firm, so healthy? We used to say, "Mom, your cheeks are like two red Delicious Apples!"
She's/we're so agitated today!

She calls me. Her legs are cold she says and she wants her blanket around her knees. This is a first for her but I wrap her favourite, yellow, hand-knit throw around her legs in bed. I notice a blotchy patch on the bed. She's becoming incontinent. She's very agitated now as she realizes she needs help to the bathroom. She reluctantly takes my arm. Then as we approach the door she quickly pushes me away and draws it shut. Her voice still strong, full of the urgency she feels in the need to be independent: "Go away, I'm ok now!" I wait 'til she opens the door again.

I hold out my hand to her. She shrugs, tries on her own. She stumbles and gives up. She takes my hand and with a deep, sad sigh, puts it loosely, grudgingly, in hers.

And I say to her, "Mom, how many times have you held out your hand for me!"

...We're both so very agitated today!

Rachel Rambling #91

They tell me I must learn to place some boundaries
That I ought not feel your pain so intensely
That I must not let YOUR pain be mine
YOUR pain that flows so deeply into MY veins

Your bones, now so brittle, your body now so frail
The bandages I wrap around you
To bring you comfort, to dull your pain
Fail us both so deeply

They tell me I must learn to place some boundaries
And yet, they tell me little else

Where are those boundaries?
How does one stem a river's flow?

They tell me I must learn to place some boundaries
But what real advice can they give me
When, like a child, I look behind the mirror
And find only YOU are there!

And so, Mom, I pray the candle lit by our symbiotic relationship
will never burn low, knowing full well that:

**Life burns down to a very tiny flame that so easily flickers
out (Rachel Carson)**

**But, that's all for another day. Mom, today it's your 101st
Birthday!!!! I'll think about it tomorrow!**

For now, Ciao, bella Mamma! Jolanda

photo courtesy of David Ainley

3. COMRADES (OUR ALLIES/ SUPPORTERS/ KIN)

Two or three things I know for sure, and one of them is that change when it comes cracks everything open. Dorothy Allison. 1995. Two or Three Things I Know for Sure. New York: Penguin Group. p. 48.

Creativity is grounded not in dreamy vagueness but in piercing clarity. We 'see' a piece of work and then we work to shape it. We 'envision' a new direction and then we move toward it. The creative journey is characterized not by a muzzy and hazy retreat from reality but by the continual sorting and reordering and structuring of reality into new forms and new relationships. Julia Cameron. 2002. Walking in This World; The Practical Art of Creativity. New York: Penguin Putnam, Inc. p. 137.

...moving toward a Thirdspace perspective and away from the narrowed channels of Firstspace and Secondspace modes of knowledge formation.

This foregrounding carries with it an unsettling epistemological [way of knowing] and theoretical critique that revolves around disruptions and disorderings: of difference, of confidently centered identities, and of all forms of binary categorization. It seeks instead a multiplicitous 'alterity,' a transgressive 'third way' that is more than just the sum or combination of an originary dualism. At its best, such critical spatial thinking seeks to undermine its own authority by a form of textural and political practice that privileges uncertainties, rejects authoritive and paradigmatic structures that suggest permanence or inviolability, invites contestation, and thereby keeps open the spatial debate to new and different possibilities. Edward W. Soja, 1996, Thirdspace: Journeys to Los Angeles and Other Real-And-Imagined Places. Oxford: Blackwell Publishers. p. 107

Consequently, the paradox of Suzanne Farrell's career [as a dancer and] as a muse involves both her rare willingness to be termed a muse and an equally uncommon situation in which the artist and his muse were genuine partners, true collaborators. In fact, both were artists of extraordinary stature, geniuses in their own right, and their partnership produced works of genius that, in all probability, neither would have created alone.

Yet interestingly, if unsurprisingly, no one...ever refers to George Balancine as Suzanne Farrell's muse; the very idea seems somehow subversive, irreverent, sacrilegious, and irreconcilable... Francine Prose, 2002, <u>The Lives of the Muses: Nine Women Artists and the Artists They Inspired</u>. Toronto: Harper Flamingo Canada. p. 302

. CLAYTON BOEHLER

. ROB BUDDE

. WILL MORIN

. CHUCK FRASER

CLAYTON BOEHLER

I have been a social worker, a feminist, and pissed off
ever since I can remember. There are some days I want to
quit (give up, throw in the towel, I'm not making a
difference, the fight is too much, too exhausting) but I can't.
My soul won't allow it. When I get down and starting
thinking about going back to simple retail, selling people
crap they don't need, my soul screams at me. It scratches
at my insides. If I don't fight for/with marginalized people,
who will? I know Gordon Campbell won't/isn't; the
capitalists won't; the patriarchs won't. It is so emotionally

and intellectually rewarding to help someone get adequate
social housing or a bed in detox. These things, and my soul,
keep me in this profession.

My appreciation and admiration of women began at
an early age with a close bond with my mother. I think this
bond develops with most boys until they reach a certain age
when society says it's 'uncool'.

My appreciation and admiration continued to grow
with the birth of my sister. I was so excited. My parents
even let me name her; Crystal Gayle, after the country
singer whose trademark is her hair that she let grow right
to the floor. Mom remembers coming into Crystal's bedroom
to find me in her crib with a blanket tucked into the back of
my shirt and Crystal with a headband and a piece of rope. I
was Superman and she was Wonder Woman and we were
going to "beat up bad guys" together. We moved to Salmon
Valley, a beautiful community about 20 minutes north of
Prince George where I've spent the last 25 years. I just
recently moved to Vancouver and have enjoyed urban
living, but secretly miss Salmon Valley.

Other writings? I keep a journal of what is going on
in my head, heart and surroundings. I have been known to
write poetry and prose. Some of which has been previously
published (but that was way back in grade 10, so we're not
gonna talk about that). I can't write unless I am inspired
and have reached an inner calmness. Then the words
and/or images flow out. I have only found two ways to
reach my inner peacefulness. The first is dancing and the
second is sitting on the toilet.

Yes, that's what I said... dancing. I know this sounds
cheesy, but dancing centers me. I love to dance. It clears
my mind and the answers I have so desperately been

searching for, suddenly appear out of the chaos that is my life.

   I am pleased, excited and honored to be a part of this work for two main reasons. First, to honor my mother. Without her love, devotion, time, passion, commitment, patience, thoughtfulness, selflessness, caring, wisdom, guidance, I wouldn't be the person I am today, and I really enjoy the person I am. She is one of two people in my life who can call me on my shit and I don't freak out.

The other reason is to acknowledge and honour women everywhere. Being a feminist has opened my eyes to the struggle of women and I feel that it is necessary to not only join that resistance (Movement), but to also pay tribute to it; to acknowledge the achievements women and their allies have made; and to encourage more[18].

The bulk of the work I have included here is from a journal I found that I started a long time ago. I read it and then made some comments to bring you up to speed.

I want you to know about one of my favorite quotes:

"Mostly they think feminism is a bunch of angry women who want to be like men. They do not even think about feminism as being about rights - about women gaining equal rights. When I talk about the feminism I know - up close and personal - they willingly listen, although when our conversations end, they are quick to tell me I am different, not like the "real" feminists who hate men, who are angry. I

---

[18] I wish to thank the following people for sharing their knowledge, energy, time, patience, love, support, music, lyrics, inspiration, and creativity; Mom, Dad, Crystal & Clarke Pollard, Matthew, Auntie Syl, Auntie Janet, Auntie Elly, Charlotte, Amber, Tori Amos, Ani Difranco, bell hooks, Si, Chuck, Catherine, Brenda, Gail, Mary, Brenda, Olive, Carleen, Theresa, Wendy and Mr. Zral.

assure them I am as real and as radical a feminist as one can be, and if they dare to come closer to feminism they will see it is not how they have imagined it." bell hooks, 2000, <u>Feminism is for Everybody</u>, Cambridge, MA: South End Press. pp vii-viii

And another favorite quote:

"I need a big loan from the girl zone" - from the song, *Caught a Lite Sneeze* by Tori Amos

April 17, 1975

Dear Diary,
I was created today. My mother's womb is nice and warm. Mom and Dad sure talk a lot. They talk about Dad's work and what they are going to do now that I'm on the way. Dad's not always here. Sometimes he leaves really early in the morning and comes home in time for supper. He does this for a bit, and then switches to leaving late in the afternoon and coming home at night. When this happens, we eat supper earlier, and then he leaves and comes back when I'm asleep. I don't get it. Mom spends a lot of time alone. She does a lot of work at home. So much work that even I start to sweat.

I keep hearing this man singing and playing something.
.....

November 10, 1975

Dear Diary;
Two ears, two eyes, one nose, one mouth, a tongue, two legs, two arms, a penis... everything's accounted for. Things are moving right along.
Grandma came all the way from Saskatchewan to help Mom with the housework and to help Mom for when I am born. So on days when Mom is too tired to cook, Grandma makes sure supper is ready for Dad and she doesn't seem to mind this at all.
I have been struggling with this urge to turn upside down. I see no purpose turning upside down will serve. Not only will all the blood rush to my head, it will just be uncomfortable. It has gotten stronger in the last couple of days and I don't think I can fight it any more.
.....

November 19, 1975

Dear Diary,
    I have this overwhelming urge to turn upside down. It doesn't make any sense. All my blood would rush to my head and that would hurt... wouldn't it Mom? Mmmm... I can feel Mom rubbing me through her belly. I like that. Mom drinks this fizzy stuff. I think I heard her call it Root Beer. Yummy! I don't like it when Mom goes outside. It's too cold, but she helps Dad shovel the driveway and feed the cows.

PS. I'm still hearing that man singing and playing something. It only seems to happen on Sunday nights. I'll keep you posted.
.....

January 23, 1976

Dear Diary,   2:06am
    What's going on? Not only has all the fluid disappeared, but also for the last couple of hours, Mom has been pushing on me really hard. I'm getting squished and my head is distorted. I knew I shouldn't have turned upside down. That was just stupid. I should have fought that urge instead of giving in.

9:47am
    I think we went for a drive, but I'm not sure. Mom's pushing on me even harder.

11:20am
    She's pushing me down this corridor, cave thing. It's like a waterslide. I can't go back, so I might as well go with it.

11:23am
    Damn it!!! It's too freakin' cold out here. I want back in. There's no way I'll ever do that again. I want my Mommy. You!... get your rubber hands off me. Screw this!!!

Looking Back,
September 15, 2002

I don't recall writing any of this. I guess if this entry is in
my journal, then I wrote it. I didn't realize how lonely Mom was
until I was putting this together. I must have been difficult for her
to be alone all day. Reading all these entries really helps me
understand what stay at home moms go through. I welcome this
learning with open arms.
.....

April 6, 1990

Dear Diary,
        Today is Mom's first day of work. A couple of months ago,
she announced that she wanted to get her drivers licence and find
a job and get some money. I think she was just tired of feeling like
she wasn't good enough or couldn't do some of the things that
other women were doing.
        Even though it was her decision to get a job, she was so
terrified and felt she didn't have any skills to offer. I'm like, "You
raised two kids, three if you count Dad. You can cook for at least
15 people with relative ease. You know how to get 'tough, ground
in stains' out. You have an infinite amount of patience. You can
do a million things at once, perfectly."
        Now that Mom has a job, the rest of the family has to 'pick
up the slack' as far as the household chores are concern.
Everybody will do his or her own laundry. Everyone will clean up
after himself or herself.
.....

Looking Back,
September 15, 2002

My mother was a stay at home mom. This was, in part, because they both wanted one parent to always be with the children and it wasn't feasible for Dad to work part time or quit his job because his job paid well. I also think the fact that Mom was taught (and she believed) she didn't have the skills to do anything else except clean the house and have supper on the table for when Dad came home from work.

At the time, I thought Mom wanted a job because, "...she was just tired of feeling like she wasn't good enough or couldn't do some of the things that other women were doing", and that may be true, but now I think she wanted to be needed. My sister and I were grown up and could look after ourselves, so there was no reason for Mom to stay at home all the time.

I always encouraged her and hoped she would broaden her horizons, but I don't think she had enough support. I mean we support her decisions, but she didn't get much support from her parents. If anything, Grandpa and Grandma were stifling her with very strict gender roles, reinforced with an extremely heavy dose of Christianity. "Welllll Clayton, that's just the way we were raised. I was raised to look after the man and Dad wasn't raised to do the cooking, cleaning and stuff." She said this a fair amount.

Everyone looking after themselves was the plan, but it didn't quite work out that way. In addition to her work outside the home, Mom still did the majority of the housework. Jobs that were not divided up among the family, either the job didn't get done or Mom did them. It was difficult. I knew we had to help out around the house, but we weren't raised with this in mind and so it was so difficult to adjust.
.....

October 6, 1990

Dear Diary,

So I finally did it. I told Mom I didn't want to go to church any more. This was incredibly difficult because my Mom is so religious. She gets it from her parents, and their parents before them and their parents before them... It's like it was <u>drilled</u> into her. Anyway, I have been feeling like this for some time, but I didn't want to hurt her feelings. We were in the kitchen and I just said it. She didn't freak out. Actually we had a really good discussion about it. I told her I couldn't understand why we have to go to a Church to talk to God. If God is as powerful as everyone says he is, then I should be able to talk to him anyway and not have to go to church. Then I asked what makes us think God is a male. Why can't God be female or an animal or an object? I told her about how the First Nations culture have many spirits and that is what I would like to move toward; less religion and more spirituality.

I told her that another reason I don't like going to church is because they're money hungry. I asked her if she remembered when the Priest said he was going to pass the collection plate around a second time because he felt we were being too stingy? And why is it necessary to have everything made out of gold? From what the Priest says, Jesus had nothing and was completely happy. So why do they need all that? She said that she had never really thought about it and that it's just the way it's always been. It's just the way it's always been. A phrase I was hearing a lot of.

The final reason I didn't like going to church was the confessional. I told Mom, "I don't understand why I have to tell some dirty ole man about all the nasty things I did that month. Again, if God is as powerful as they say he is, I don't need this 'middleman'." Then after I tell the Priest all my deep dark secrets, as pennance, he tells me, to go say some prayers. To me prayers are just a bunch of words strung together that I rattle off without even thinking about. And how is this making me a better person?

I don't have to go to church anymore.

Looking Back,
September 15, 2002

After that conversation, I think Mom realized just how much negative influence the church had on her. She went to a school were the nuns were her teachers and she said they were not very nice. They reinforced the stereotype that men belong outside in the fields and women belong in the house to cook, clean, and raise the kids. Mom was raised to not question her elders and here I am questioning everything. I think this gave Mom the opportunity to re-evaluate why she goes to church.

We had several conversations about religion after this main one. She was worried that I was "straying away from God", I said I wasn't. I was just leaving the church and organized religion. I kept saying that we don't need all these middlemen. We can talk to God one on one. I said that I believe that my conscience is God telling me what is right and wrong; what I should and should not be doing.

As the years went on, my sister stopped going and so did my parents. Mom still prays and talks to God, sometimes too much. Crystal, Dad, and I tease her about bugging God so much. We firmly believe that they are on a first name basis. Mom's perception of God has definitely changed, and for the better I think. She too has embraced the idea that we do not need "the middle man" to communicate to God. She believes that the church, the priests in particular, were just grabbing power, "I have to go tell a man my sins in order to get to heaven. It's bullshit."
.....

September 15, 2002

Dear Diary,
My mother and I still have some of the most in depth and intense conversations...
Since this journal, I received my Bachelor of Social Work. So now I can articulate the feminist movement and how that applies to my mother. For example when we are talking about members of

our family and she cannot understand why this person would do such a thing, I am able to point out various motivations or outside forces with the help of my feminist courses, books and people in my life.

Mom continues to work in the health care field where a new challenge has emerged, ageism. There is a rumour circulating that some of the women's contracts will not be renewed because of their age. Granted it's just a rumour, but it's enough to get my mother riled up.

She also helps Dad in his 'field'. She can throw a bail of hay just as well as Dad and she single-handedly saved the lives of at least two calves.

I think my mother is one of the most amazing women I know. More and more women from her generation are breaking the 'norms' and attaining something better for them. Yet, there are still some women who find it much easier to comply with patriarchy and don't challenge the male dominated workforce, gender roles, or religion as my mother has and continues to. As my mother used to say, "It's easier for me to change me, than to change the world." I wonder if she realizes that she is changing the world.

I asked Mom if she thought she was a feminist. She laughed and said no. I guess you could say my mother is a closet feminist. She is constantly empowering those who feel powerless, challenging homophobia, sexism, and ageism. My mother has accomplished so much in her time and she continues to achieve things that, at one point in her life, she didn't think were possible. My sister and I hope Mom will acknowledge her accomplishments and triumphs. Something she has difficulty doing. Maybe this book will help her do that.

P.S. That man playing the guitar on Sunday nights... Tommy Hunter.
.....

Even in Pain*

PAIN! PAIN! PAIN!
"Tell Lucy what happened, but don't alarm her."
(Even in pain, you still care about others)

PAIN! PAIN! PAIN!
"I have a meeting with Sarah. Could you call her and tell her I won't be there."
(Even in pain, you are still considerate of others)

PAIN! PAIN! PAIN!
"My husband should at the gym right now."
(Even in pain, you still know where your husband is)

PAIN! PAIN! PAIN!
"My keys are in my coat pocket. My son can have my car."
(Even in pain, you are still a mother)

PAIN! PAIN! PAIN!
"Thanks you guys for being here"
(Even in pain, you still remember to thank us)

Gentle, kind, soft-spoken, genuine, tender, open-mind, open-heart, peaceful, soothing, warm, caring, compassionate, thoughtful, sensitive, welcoming, helpful, fiery, persistent, challenging, thought provoking, insightful, artistic, aboriginal, beautiful, joyful, woman, strong, courageous, independent, solid, spiritual, reliable, trusting, honest...

I use these words to describe you.

*Dedicated to Catherine Baylis. (April 2002)
.....

After Thought

Congratulations on getting that published.
In the paper, you know how you were writing about how the
creative process helped you in understanding yourself? Well that
got me thinking about how this process helped me understand,
not only myself, but also my mother and other women who had
similar experiences as my mother. i.e. stay at home moms.

When I was growing up, being a 'writer' or getting published
wasn't a thought for me. It wasn't that I thought it would never
happen, or that it wasn't an option. The thought just wasn't
there. So, I have to thank you for providing this creative
opportunity for self-growth.

Once I found this 'unknown option', I started looking for others.
The biggest one I found was, "I could be a social worker in
London, England." That revelation was almost too big to
comprehend. After I said it, I laughed out loud. Then I laughed at
my own shock and astonishment.

As I said before, this process helped me understand my mother
and what she went through. At the time, I didn't understand the
depth of the loneliness and isolation she went through. I guess
that was because I was self-absorbed as most teenagers are.

I call my parents every Thursday at 7 p.m. and this time I told
Mom I understood what she went through raising my sister and
me. At first she just brushed it off, like it was nothing or just a
part of being a mom. I went through some of the emotions she
went through, and she grew quiet. Then I apologized. I don't know
why. Maybe it was for me. Maybe it was for her. Maybe it was on
behalf of patriarchy. I don't know. I wish it didn't have to be that
way. I wish I had done something sooner. I guess this is just
another example of how patriarchy lets everybody down.

I hope these revelations don't ever stop. Reaching a deeper
understanding of what women have gone through and continue to
go through will greatly benefit my practice. When I'm working

with a female client, we will be able to move forward at a much faster pace if she doesn't have to struggle to explain where she is coming from and what she's feeling.

I hope the men who read this book will take a moment and think about it. Think about patriarchy; about feminism; about violence; about their relationship with women; about their relationship with men. Who is benefiting from those relationships? Who is hindered? Who has the power? Who doesn't? And why? Getting men to think about these thinking is just another goal I have for this book.

.....

ROB BUDDE

I am a student of language and a teacher of empowerment and awareness through creative writing. I am fundamentally and profoundly dissatisfied with the world: its injustices, its dishonesty, its violences, its toxic structures of institutional power. I have had female/feminist mentors both on and off the page: my

mother Laura Budde who grows all things green, Aritha van
Herk whose personal power altered my sense of the writing
academic, bell hooks who taught me teaching as a practice
of freedom, Dionne Brand who taught me revolution is
possible against a North American racist, sexist 'common
sense,' Nicole Brossard who taught me the value of writing
an aerial desire that spiraled out of sense, Debbie Keahey,
my partner, who took me by the hand to an underground
river of awareness beyond theory, beyond writing, beyond
knowing anything, and finally, my daughters, Robin and
Erin, who continually pull me from my structured self,
mock my pretenses, see right through those useless
trappings of contemporary life like 'career,' 'success,' and
'meetings.' All these wise and powerful women have made
me into this, a male-in-progress, troubled, doubled,
doubting, wanting more, wanting out of patriarchy,
knowing how much hard work that will take.

flicker #1

georgio o'keefe was not a naturalist and she was not mad. she was in love.

it is hard to think of your mother as 'in love'. hard to imagine that kind of inner life in a woman who has had such an overwhelming role on your life.

a friend once watched entranced as my mother pruned back a grape ivy. "she is in ecstasy," she whispered to me across the kitchen table. i remember then thinking of my mother's flower garden. a riot of lip, moisture-laden tendril, pollen, gentle sinews which curve and lounge against the sun. the latent burst of a bulging poppy bud. the undulations of green flesh lapping against our angular house. i was reeling.

with a half-smile, a wistful private warmth, my mother presses the hot loamy earth around a transplanted foxglove. it is just after dawn and the morning glories are beginning to untwine. visibly they unfold out, like some ocean anemone.

her gardens were never riotous. she could have had riotous gardens. i once thought only madwomen had riotous gardens but now i know that's not true. her gardens were unruly within their boundaries; clumps and sweeps of growth twined and crested against each other: cheers of daisy, spumes of lily, undercurrents of patience and baby's breath.

my garden is scattered and beleaguered; the weeds invading, large stretches unplanted, septembers without blooms. desire unkempt, incoherent. i am young, still learning how desires exist in the things you do, the way you co-exist with other living things that stand for love. my mother comes in from the greenhouse, peat still on her hands, to give advice, suggest seeds, talk rain onto the horizon.

flicker #2

it was absurd. our crystalline arrangement manic and gorgeous. the rope tugged at my waist. we shuffled with baby steps through powdered snow like dust. my father wanted to test the river ice and we set out from shore with a heavy crowbar to chip away at doubts. step step chunk step step chunk. i stood twenty feet behind, a frayed yellow rope the umbilical cord between us. even now, looking back, it seemed an unearthly journey; father and son joined at the waist over distance, anchor and lead, the treacherous ice, the faint tracks, the ponderous, subterranean flow of black water below. step step chunk.

it might as well have been shifting sand, a boom of logs, a field of sea, the landscape carried us away but any would do. the ice was ours, momentary, flexing, dear. step step chunk. my eyes were on the rope between us, the rope tensing and slack, our tracks revealing obsidian ice, fissures and creases, the slick sky reflected back. creaks and groans floated up as if the dead were stirring below. suddenly, the rush of possibilities welled up, my hands, blue with cold, gripped the rope tighter. step step chunk step. and the possibilities splintered. shards flew against my tongue.

so easy it would be for both of us to be lost. a great chasm yawning black beneath our feet, distance made irrelevant by sheer force, we would flail, be driven under, shocked to silence by the cold. weightless, words would leave us. ice cracking the rush of our lungs, colours of the sun shattered above, lost in a green-gold spiral exploding. perhaps, tied as we were, we would bump into each other, perhaps touch as we drifted down into the dark. maybe our last thought, breath gone, would be of one another.

or, upon the crack and burst of black water, the rope would sing epic in my arms. i would not go under. i would pull my father from the nothingness we seek. gasping, plunge myself against his momentum, into his wrist-grip. the iron bar would be lost, swallowed by a whale or a ghost. we would untie the rope before it turned to stone, return home, the river an eddy, a swirl of memory.

or, tirelessly, we would walk the ice with the sky endlessly turning. we would walk on. tied. the possibilities ringing in our heads. together. the far shore vanishing. step step chunk step step chunk.

oh father, what have we done? what have we done?

flicker #3

Laura loved spinning. Or is love the right word? Not just dance-like spinning, stayed and safe--she liked clattering merry-go-rounds, the random, careening twirl of her body, or someone holding her wrists spinning until both were dizzy and near nausea. Spinning until she was disoriented, staggered, out of control, like a story you can't find yourself in. And I would spin Laura--at first in an amphitheater of pillows and padding but then, gradually, the back yard, or the living room despite the corners and sharp angles. She begged, demanded, bartered her way into a spin. A sparkling prospect always it ended in a dizzy heap with regret deep in our stomachs. Sometimes that is what love is when you are seven years old. Caroming into my arms, the plea always ended to begin with "dad used to spin me." Pattern, habit, comfort--sometimes home is pure break-neck speed.

One swirling summer evening Laura was typing a letter to me, fitfully, reaching in to see where the letters come from and getting ink everywhere. With a start she jerked back with a perfect 'u' typed on her little finger. She grinned, wide-eyed with the idea of words on her skin. Beaming, she showed me her 'u'. Her eyes were on her finger. I was dizzy watching her eyes. I was the 'u' so proudly wrapped around her little finger. I was the 'u'. Dizzy.

The spinning ended one afternoon, a school holiday and no cartoons, ended with a whack against a bookcase edge, her ankle bruising deep almost before it struck. She cried long and hard. She cried for all the possible bruises, all the imagined, subtle, invisible bruises. She cried for all the threatened bruises. She cried for all the bruises only she could see. She cried for all the bruises, for all the kids, for all the world banged against he edge of a bookcase. She cried because the spinning would stop too. She cried because the spinning would stop and I would leave. She cried because the regret deep in her stomach would go on and on.

Now, far away, composing this on my computer, I type the letter 'u' like a soft pillow-padded landing but feel vertigo wash over me anyway, regret deep in my spinning stomach, terrified that some day a purple welt will appear beneath my fingers.

flicker #4

That is very surprising, my three-month-old daughter tells me with her eyes. The arch of her eyebrows, the searching blue around her big pupils pulsing with the world's sparkling new sheens, her startled spread of hands telling me in a question, this is very surprising. She is telling me, reminding me of the absolute sacred moments of the first. She is teaching me that the world is about surprise and that when the world ceases to be a surprise, we die, to be surprised somewhere else.

Often it is the strangest things that surprise her. The sound of change in someone's pocket, the gold around the eraser on a pencil, the reflection of herself in my glasses. The surprise is a blend of responses that flit across her little face in tiny bursts, like lines of a small precious poem.

Astonishment is the first part of the surprise. Astonishment that such a thing exists, the vertigo of new information falling with a swirl into her catalogue of experiences. It is the tingle of newly used senses, an opening up to a wider and wider vista, like a secluded valley slowly coming into view. A new world coming into view.

A moment of fear causes her to look at me, just a quick sidelong glance to see if I see it too. I do. I will protect her from it if it is dangerous. She follows my eyes back to it and proceeds.

Then finally, curiosity pulls her hand to it. The pencil dips and bobs, moves close enough to grasp and her hand launches out toward it, inaccurate, insistent, reverent. The curiosity is what places her in the world, pulls the pencil from the words, forces the world to look back, look up from its myopic attention on ending the poem perfectly.

flicker #5

She did not know how to work a book. That most basic of human machines and she did not know how to work it. My new daughter struggled to see what was so special. I looked up from her impatience in my lap to take a new look at the bookshelves upon bookshelves around us. I had never though about a book before. About the physical mechanics of reading.

A book to a baby is not something to read. First and foremost it is something to taste. She mouths the spine and corners with her burgeoning little incisors. Paper and board do not taste particularly good but when she is teething anything to rub against the gums is adequate. I often wonder if we don't continue to teethe against books later in life--grinding them against our sores and working our wisdom teeth out into the air. Enamel original sin.

She also liked the edge of the pages. She would flip through them over and over. The book is an object first, with physical properties. It has heft, textures, smells, edges and surfaces. It also rips. There is no sanctity in a book for her. The sound of paper ripping is far more stimulating that anything the little black patterns might have to offer.

Then she discovered that it opened but took a while longer to learn that it sadly opens only in one way. She would try and try to open it from the top or the bottom or the left side. This was frustrating for her, almost as frustrating as learning that you cannot open a book while kneeling on it. This was related to her discovery that the book changed size when you opened it. What was one page suddenly became two. You needed space to open it fully and often that was a problem. (She had this same problem with doors--trying to open them with her body in the way.)

Now she is at the stage where she is using the book herself, paging through it, making sounds at each scene, imitating our reading to her. Colours and shapes still attract more than words but she is noticing the words that adults seem to focus on. She is growing up.

But I do hope she holds onto her fascination with the book, the thing called a book. I hope that later she will pick up

her favourite and feel its weight, slide her liquid hands over the
paper, and forget about the stories for a while.

flicker #6 (for Donna Szöke)

in a railwalking silkscreen you told me you lived with
three musicians. one played percussion, thrumming in your chest
late at night. one played strings, the harp mostly, especially when
you were in love and didn't want him to. the last played light,
blended shades, angles, shadow in motion against walls, bonzai
trees, bodies. but this too is melody, the form holding only for a
time, holding back transcendence, and then you must leave. (a
plain look, open
across the distance between rails we walked parallel
conversations, balanced between two cities, between art and love,
between anger and)
then you told me that lovenergy accumulates, not the
emotion but the motion, the poems and paintings and songs, the
performance of love. either making love or making art with
friends, touching on canvas, in collage, in collusion, its
physicality leaving traces on skin. (that then is love, when
our insteps became sore from railwalking late. not
thinking about the trust of footing as we tried walking with eyes
closed until i said something, my thin voice balanced between,
and you looked, thrown off by my)
space, space to work was what you demanded, a medium
through which you moved, moved through and through, and out
again, contained or uncontested, through to skin (and the hand's
surprise
at your suggestion of joining hands across our balance, a
third center it seemed and we were both amazed at the precision
even without eyes, even despite love, formless, even) despite

flicker #7

where gender implodes, love takes up the
slack, the play, the free air.
writing love and the personal political steals away into
academic corners; it is what we are not what we do.
fall 1990 and a female grad student colleague cannot hold
her cup of coffee from shaking. her supervisor had just placed
centuries of white male approval, placed the weight of
institutional structural memory, placed his overcoded desires
squarely on her tired being.
he placed his hand on her leg in his office.
the office in this poem stands for the
status quo. the leg stands for the parts of us lost. the hand
stands for the continual re-confirmation of male power and
privilege. the shaking stands for recognition and struggle. the
stories told that day (a long day, much coffee, tears, oaths, much
silence too, shame, anger, a way out, a re-entering) stand for
revolution. we sit a while longer, talk about language and the way
symbols work.

flicker #8

the meeting room hushed. i was taken aback.
"but rob, you are still a man," she said evenly, without
malice.
delusions are meant to be dispelled.
"yes, yes, i am." i finally spoke. my disavowed self stepped
quietly back into the room. my fake self left. a man's body, a
man's history now sat at the table. my body re-entered itself at
that moment. i am still a man. that is what i have to work with.
i leaned in, got to work.

flicker #9

It had something to do with power, power and threat, and
my body seemed to know just what to do. Perhaps a defensive
mechanism, perhaps an aggressive act, marking territory.
Whatever its reason, still today, every time I walk into a bookstore
or library, I have the urge to shit.

One might laugh, but early on in my undergraduate days
it was quite disconcerting. It was confusing, like that adolescent
growth of pubic hair or that first ejaculation. What was this!? It
took me a while to figure out the pattern. At first I thought it was
just a favourite bathroom stall in the main campus library. It had
stone facing and old style toilets--made one feel important sitting
there, learned and dignified. But then I realized it was any library,
and bookstores too--any large collection of books. I thought that
maybe it was the smell of ink and paper--that sharp dusty smell
like fresh carbon paper, fire, wood shavings like they were just
spat out from a buzz-saw.

But no, no, that didn't hold up. Be damned if I was going
to reduce it to some elaborate psychoanalytic neurosis, I thought
nervously.

My slightly embarrassing bodily response to books
coincided with my early attempts at poetry. They were bad poems
about farms, love, and love on the farm. Even after I began
writing regularly and publishing some, I still responded the same
way when faced with those stacks and stacks of books.

It could have been the immensity of it--the sheer volume
and oppressive weight of all those words simply squeezing the
shit right out of me. Or scaring the shit out of me. Like the
prisoner due to be executed, might I be evacuating my bowels out
of sheer terror? Or maybe I'm like the ape who freaks out in front
of a class full of school-kids and starts flinging shit and semen all
over the place. The semen flying will have to wait for another
story but certainly there is something to fear in the vast entirety
of the book-world. It is a world of markings, territories, violence
and hurt.

I have entered that landscape of squat bundles of paper. I,
now, lay claim to a couple of books in that endless jostling queue
of anxious utterances. Now, when I enter a library, I think about

finding unknown ground, private spaces, places where others have not gone. I think about dropping all pretense and letting it fly.

WILL MORIN

Will Morin is of Ojibwa/Scottish and French Canadian ancestry, a member of the Michipicoten First Nation and originally from Batchawana Bay, Ontario. Born in Sault Ste. Marie in 1964 Will grew up mostly in Sudbury but he has travelled throughout Canada and the United States in pursuit of the creative spirit.

Will has been exhibiting his unique mixture of media and culturally inspired works and performances continually locally, nationally and internationally. Among them are exhibiting in annual national Native Art shows at the Woodlands Cultural Centre in Brantford Ontario as well as performing with Juno nominated Native Rock band No Reservations. He has won many awards at the Algoma Fall

Festival of the Arts in the past few years including "Best of the Show" twice.

Will is very active in the community and participates in local festivals and other art and cultural events. Some of them are the Northern Lights Festival Boreal, Fringe Nord Theatre Festival, and others. Will has strong organizing skills putting together arts events on a regular bases. He also has been involved with the boards of directors of the Sudbury Arts Council, and Theatre Cambrian in Sudbury. With Theatre Cambrian Will directed a World Premiere of a revised version of the 60's rock musical Hair entitled Hair Y2K with special arrangement of the co-author James Rado. To top this off every month since 1998 Will organizes and displays local artists' works at a local café / magazine store called Black Cat Too. This provides other artists and performers to get exposure and experience in public presentations of their art. Will is also a host of "Anishinaabeg This Week" a weekly one hour First Nations news magazine program for Z-103 (local radio station).

He received his formal art training first at Cambrian College and then from the Nova Scotia College of Art and Design and obtained his degree of Fine Art in 1993. Will followed this up with a degree in Native Studies from Laurentian University in 1994. Following that he began teaching at Cambrian College in the their visual arts program. Two years later he was briefly at Sault College teaching in the Four Seasons Anishinaabe Art Journey program. Will obtained an Inter-disciplinary Humanities Master's degree from Laurentian in the summer of 2001.

Will has helped to develop a new university level private art school, the White Mountain Academy of the Arts, in Elliot Lake while working as Assistant Director of Cultural Affairs. In the fall of 2001 Will began teaching the

White Mountain Academy of the Arts. Will also organized two consecutive conferences of Native Elders, Artists and Crafts people before he left Elliot Lake. Another of his projects during his time in Elliot Lake was to create a Native college / university entrance program called Mamawesen Training Institute. The fall of 2000 marked its official launch and articulation with Algoma University.

Will has co-ordinated a culturally based literacy program this past year at the N'swakamok Native Friendship Centre in Sudbury. In January 2001 and spring 2002 Will was the featured artist on two different episodes of Aboriginal Voices, on the Aboriginal Peoples Television Network. For the past two years Will has facilitated the healing benefits of art through many activities with his Creative Self Rediscovery workshops for community agencies, cultural groups, provincial aboriginal youth organizations, health professionals, and nursing students.

In contrast to his art training Will has spent most of his youth in the cadets and part of his early adult years in the reserves and the Canadian Armed forces. During the Oka Crisis and the Gulf War of 1990-91 Will served as a medical assistant in eastern Canada.

"When it comes to the art I create, I find it difficult to sell for personal, spiritual and philosophical reasons. I hope to avoid getting caught up in the viscous cycle of exploitation and commercialisation of Native Art, Native cultures, artists, and other minorities. Coming from a life of making do with what I had, I realized the connection I've made in the work to the spiritual philosophy of my Anishinaabe and Celtic ancestry. And that being everything is connected, nothing is wasted. For me, it was to recycle, reuse anything to make art."

I am a Man

The verdict is in; I committed a sin, a sin.
There was no contest; I failed an invisible test again, and again.
The verdict is in; I committed a sin, a sin.
I hold my own and sit alone in harmony as I begin, I begin.

I was accused that I didn't care, didn't care.
The jury did declare I was guilty as air, as err.
And with a scare the judge did think it was fair.
So in defense I tried to make sense of it some how somewhere.

Their hysterical logic gave consent of what they wanted and what
they meant.
I couldn't debate her, that walking stenographer, what they said
wasn't what I meant.
I assessed the emotional reasoning for their dissent, what they
said wasn't what I meant.
And in their cross-examination came the point of her summation,
what I felt was irrelevant

But sometimes a fuck is just a fuck in Freudian style you see.
Yet when it isn't just that, it becomes a conspiracy,
That is authored for me and oblivious to me.
The verdict is in; I committed a sin, by being me

This is not a bashing of women or even men.
It is stating the obvious to you an unconditional friend.
That I was lost in a relationship I could not end,
And lost where I was going and where I've been.

Therefore, this I understand, I have been labeled, I am a man.
And it isn't a birth rite or a disability or my ego taking a stand.
Yes, I am, I am a man, and this I understand.
I am not the victim and I am not the victimizer at someone else's
hand.

Raising your voice in anger or frustration is not exclusive to a
gender role.

And neither is being a prick even if you don't have a phallic power pole.
I have a penis and a soul, a mind and sometimes I am emotional.
So I profess to be non-compromising and yet accused of being conditional.

Each of these parts of me is sensitive, reachable and all ways in flux.
I like sex after talking and like talking after sex.
I am not denying my guilt in all I built or am I milking my innocence,
And being so bold as to hold such a view is either an excuse or my defense.
This I understand, I am more than just a man.
I am not a lady, or slim shady, I am a Hue Man.
The verdict is in; I committed a sin, a sin.
I hold my own and sit alone in harmony as I begin, I begin.

......

Leaves Falling Moon

September in the Ojibway language is literally 'Leaves Changing Moon', the beginning of harvest time. September's 'Leaves Changing Moon' precedes October's 'Leaves Falling Moon'. The ushering in of colour change and cooler weather excites me. In this dying season is the energy of my birth. The smells of cool leaf rot and the rustling of brittle amber paper scraps are yet to come. Through these heightened senses these letters of bloom lift my spirit as they prepare to descend and paint the earthen canvas.

On the eve of my 38th birth celebration I disrobe the years of camouflages with the falling of each leaf as my true self is exposed to the cold dry winds. In anticipation of the impending nakedness I dive into the idea of letting go, of declaring my flaws, professing my excuses and writing an affirmation. In the tradition of St. Augustine and Rene Decarte's confession, I masturbate my ego and liberate my soul. The hardest thing to do is keep the fear

of what others would think close by as I emancipate the power of
thought, the pain of experience and wisdom in death.

.....

Never Too Much

Birthed into a paradox I stand between a parallax of world views
that fluctuates with the seasons where nature knew
what the question was and those who didn't have a clue.

Birthed into a paradox would I be too answered to ask why
if I was too blind to speak, too deaf for my eyes,
would I be too vocal to hear, too quiet to cry?

This self-inflected social dilemma sparked me to ponder
Maybe I am too selfish to hoard, too generous to bother
too smart to know, too aware to be stupid like the father.

Did I appear too rich to spend, too poor to save my soul,
too proud to change, too strong to feel the whole,
leaving me too happy to hurt or too brave to kill the toll.

Or was I too hungry to eat, too full to fast and fray,
too alone to meat, too crowded to flee away
and too lost to be found while being too saved to pray?
Did I look too rested to stand, too tired to sleep,
too asleep to dream, too awake to think what to keep
while being too bored to yawn or weep?

Have you decided if I was too discontented to loath,
too dissatisfied to condemn or that life was too precious to hold,
or too extreme to balance and too paradoxical to grow old?

Or is it up to you to say when it is too little too late
and too much too little of what I give and what I ate
adding to the "to be or not to be, to think or not to think" debate?

While you think about it I will drink a little too much from a good
thing,
And out of sight beyond your institutional eyes where I will dance
and sing.
Ask me and maybe I'll share a sip of this natural thing.

Birthed into a paradox I stand between a parallax of this natural
thing.
Birthed into a paradox I stand between a parallax of this natural
thing.

.....

For Women: Part 1

Forgive me women for what I am about to say.
I am a man,
a product
of a
left brain,
narrow
phallic
view
of the
world,
who is
on TOP,
in Control.

That I have a socially accepted rite of passage to be a savage.
My lying lion sir-loins will say or do anything to get some.
I have a brain in two places, right now I could be wearing two
faces.
One that is weak and brittle, the other is blind and selfish.
I want your breast in my mouth, like a child at your chest.
Forgive me Mother, for I am a Man.

Part 2
...because I have been Mez more eyezed. The shame of it, the
socially, religious taboo of it, the strongest natural force on earth.
It ain't a volcano, or a wild animal, it ain't political systems or the
knowledge you have. It lies next to you and lies to be released on
you. It consumes us all. We are its result, its victim, its prey.
Without it we would surely
die. Because of it some of us will die. What is it? I ask you, what
is it?

When I was younger and knew it all, I had tunnel vision to my
needs with my head up my butt. What I didn't know was that it
was devouring my mind and soul. It was a physical need de-
evolving me to a primal state of desire.

Today, right now I just caught myself admiring the curves of a
woman's
thigh, herrrrr....! Butt, but, her mind is further up, look up, come
on,
LOOK UP, up ? way up..............but, her butt, I can't. Ooooh, the
way
the fabric hugs her, lies across her. Wait! Why do I? Why am I
sooohoo?,
why can't I just....?

Huh, why am I so easily distracted at the sight of a woman?
Why do I become so detached for those few sex, huh, I mean
seconds?

The air between her and me draws me back to a distant reality.
Ohh, she's ten feet in front of me. I want to see her naked and feel
the curves of her butt, her lower back, her shoulders, her neck,
her hair, oooohhhh and her face. I want to draw with my finger
the lines my eyes see.

Why do I want this? Can anyone tell me this? Why!? Why did I
want my mother's breast in my mouth? Now I want yours. Why
does it feel so good to see them bare before me? What do I get
from this when I am lactose intolerant? Why does it feel so good

when I see you, feel you, lie next to you, hold you, am inside you?
Can you tell me, why? Freud comes to mind but where is he now?
Dead.

Mother, take me back. Return me to the warmth of your insides
where I can hear the calming beat of your heart. My insatiable
fetal needs consume me and I never have anything to give. Or do
I? What do I give you, what do I give her? Love? Is there love in
this eco-ystem of ego and gender instability?

My needs are mostly emotional buried beneath layers of time,
guilt, shame
and systemic abuse man-festing into physical responses of;
desire, anger
and fear. Man's Trinity.

I am still a child, I am not fully developed, I'm not
complete.Mother take me back! (The sound of a drum beating
assists my rebirth)

Part 3
Forgive me men for I am a man,
in touch with my feminine side,
and it feels good? to be in balance
Mentally, Physically, Emotionally and Spiritually.
I don't need to call out for mom. I don't need a breast in my
mouth. I've weaned myself with the aid of feminine energy
that instinctively cared without condition. Just think,
unconditional love.
Unlike that man up there in that hierarchy whose mission is
imposition
spewing an illusion through confusion.
"I know the way! He can save the day."
And as he punctuates with a fist,

"Jesus is coming! Are you prepared?!"

The only thing that comes to mind is anal sterility.
Get your suppositories here, suppositories for the Physically,

Mentally, Spiritually constipated. Right now, only a buck. And if
you need help getting up there,
you know where,

"Ask and you shall receive!"

But I ask for nothing and get it all.
I take nothing until I've given first.
My needs are few.
Do you know that we have been deceived?
I can no longer believe,
it is time to bereave
your death, and move on.

Forgive me Father. I can no longer follow you.

.....

Mother

If I were blind, an orphan or worse,
a babe at your breast ready to nurse.
I would have to reach for more than a book,
for something that needs a 2nd, 3rd & 4th look.
I'd then try to feel each line, building a world in my mind,
of worlds out of reach at the tip of my fingers,
with imaginary lands, between them lingers.
I'd feel the character's hearts and souls.Painting for me pictures
whole.
Centuries past with futures to come,
the smell of sweat, a women's humm.
Aaaah, the taste of her sweat and the thrust of pleasure.
The sight of blood, that of another.
Then the taste of that blood and the thrust of its pain,
from cold steel through her veins

Lives pass but souls remain, with the smell of roses,
the thrust of thorns, than blood again.

Now, if I knew my name or mother at least,
I wouldn't be blind, orphaned or a beast.

Who ever, What ever, Where ever you may be,
Mother, I am sorry.

.....

Passion-ate.

Ohh passionate me, ohh passion ate me.
Can't you see, it consumed me.
Com passion ate with me.

I am passionate about the air, the sky, the smell of change and
the sensation of a rain drop as it slowly winds it way down my
bare skin. I am captivated with the bond between a child and a
toy, the slow desire a tree has for the sun, and the drive of our
foot on the gas peddle of life. The sight of pollen woos me as it
floats softly into my site and lifts my imagination to a feathered
place of soft skin and silky hair.

Ohh passionate me, ohh passion ate me.
Can't you see, it consumed me.
Com passion ate with me.

I admire couples that take long walks together and I would smile
when a pair of these wrinkled hands slowly swing together as
they painly, arthritically move through the day with a calm well
spoken silence and warm kisses.

Ohh passionate me, ohh passion ate me.
Can't you see, it consumed me.
Com passion ate with me.

I crave to create deep within the loins of my muse and pulse-ate
passion on canvas with paint and orgasm as my fingers vibrate
across the fibers of the tight cotton surface now liquid smooth

sensually spelling colorful thoughts about the mixing of ideas, in
analogues and harmonious gentle curves that match the shape of
a woman's lips, her smile, her hair, her eyes, of you in liquid
motion of slow sensual swirls that go to work in the mind's eye to
my soul.

Ohh passionate me, ohh passion ate me.
Can't you see, it consumed me?
Com passion ate with me.

I am passion-ate on the dance floor where we'd swim, slip and
slide in each other's arms to the sweat that baths our bodies and
brace one another when we stumble and dive deep within each
other.

I am passion-ate between the covers of your eyes, and between
the sheets of musical notes you sing to.

I am passion-ate about the places I go when the music rockets me
to another pure realm, a deeper depth, a cosmic chaos of creative
processes.

I am passion-ate in all I do and I celebrate with those who join
me.

I invite you, welcome you, defend you and commend you for
having passion-ate with me. Thanks.

.....

Dis-spell, miss-spell the mythos

Dis-spell, miss-spell the mythos of everyone's words void of
connections to
the past, to relation-ships in the present and bonds to the fu fu fu
fu forever
process of life.

The 7 shaaaaakraaaasssss of bastard economics in its reality of material
success hangs value like a cross from egos known noun of none-things.

.....

Justify.

I justify myself to release and relieve my guilt. I mislead you, abuse you and release my guilt. I profess, lead me not into temptation, cause it can find me itself. You see, its all around us showering me with golden urine rain through the eye of my pain, a window inside out and framed in guilt. My phallic ego masturbate me through you to justification. Here I gooh ahh, I gooh ahh I give
you my guilt.
No need to thank me. It was nothing more than what was done to me. It was nothing really. I'm just sharing it with you now to keep up the tradition. Passin' it on as it were.

Again, no need to thank me. It's the least I can do in my insatiable need to release my guilt. But I am not trying to be rude as others are better at it than I am.

They are the ones who raped me to relieve their blue balls of guilt in order to justify themselves. Even though someone else set the fire they inherited this tradition and made it their mission and we were burnt. However, when it came to take the blame there they were and then there they weren't.
They relieved their guilt by sticking their dicks into my ears ejaculating prematurely leaving behind V. D., a Virtual Dis-ease for power positions, power figures, power situations and power symbols.

They abused me, used me and gave me their guilt. Now I give to you.

Wait - a - second. I am starting to see a pattern through the
smoke of deception.
I don't like what I see! Hey! I don't like this tradition.

Ya, You up there. Do you really care?
What are you hiding behind that mask?
No more like before! Next time, I ask,
see that I am trying to respect myself by listening to others.
Next time, I ask, see that I am trying to respect myself.
Next time, I ask, see that I am trying to respect.
Next time, I ask, see that I am trying.
Next time, I ask, see that respect.
Next time, I ask, see that.
Next time, I ask, see.
Next time, ask!

.....

Etched in Sandstone

Etched in sandstone
and sealed with silicone,
I will never be
old enough to be
so wise as to think
I was young enough
to know it all.
Etched in sandstone
and sealed with silicone.

.....

She Brings

She brings a smile
lit with happiness,
that conjures up
thoughts and fantasies
from the many facets
and mysteries of her life.

Leaving no limits
to where she's been or where she's going.

Having no boundaries
of who she was or what
she's becoming.

In flight she fights

her fears,
her frights
of being alone.

She brings a smile
lit with happiness
no one else can own.

.....

CHUCK FRASER

I could not imagine a world without women/ feminisms. When I see flowers, matters not a rose, dandelion, or cactus, they are all special and each has value, I'm reminded of women. Flowers, like women, offer hope, beauty, peace, and life. I'm especially fond of wild flowers, they grow free and unhindered, as all things and people were meant to be. Self-actualization is a sign of full bloom. In order for people to achieve this metamorphous, there must be a world free from constraints like: patriarchy, racism, oppression, violence, poverty, and greed. These are some reasons I consider myself an ally and friend to women.

As a social activist on many fronts for 25 years I've had the privilege of working with many sisters. I'm encouraged by the struggle of the women's movement, for it is such determination that will one day allow us to live on a planet of peace and harmony. There is little choice but to organize progressive groups to work in cooperation to take back Mother Earth from the evil powers of globalization and nurture her back to health.

I consider it a Highland honour to be a participant in such an endeavour as this project. If it had not been for the women I've encountered along my sojourn, I would not be the man I am today. Poetry shared in this book is a reflection of some women who've influenced me to take a stance for altruistic social justice and to have become an ally in the struggle for a more caring and compassionate world.

My solo mother raised four children, one year apart. Later with the assistance of my grandfather and grandmother, she put herself through nursing school. Mom worked as a practical nurse at the Winnipeg General Hospital, in the maternity ward, on the midnight shift for 25 years.

My Maori partner/soul mate, Tina, has been my main supporter. We have shared the last 25 years together. Tina is my best friend and the mother to my children. We've raised three children of our own, and cared for 75 children as foster parents over the last seventeen years. Together we have lived a life of diversity. Our youngest son Brandon was born with Down Syndrome, autism, and is legally blind, as well as being non-verbal. He is our Budda.

My two daughters: Rhiannon (25) and Tessa (20) are the sunshine in my life. Rhiannon and her partner Chris have given us two grandchildren. Tessa is in college and wants to become a social worker. Both have given me great joy and inspiration.

I will share poems about local women in the Prince George area that have also given me inspiration and hope for a better day. On the picket lines, peace marches, and protests, I value the solidarity developed with the many sisters in the struggle for a more just and humane society. I dedicate my part of this poetry book to all the women I have known and who helped me to learn about love and compassion. As an egalitarian male I will forever be thankful.

In my life I've been: son, brother, grandson, uncle, boyfriend, husband, lover, nephew, grandfather, father, teacher, ally, counsellor, advocate, god father, structural social worker, blue collar worker, student, and working class poet. I've been truly blessed. Peace & Love.

Who does own the fragrance of flowers, certainly not the arrogance of man, of that I'm sure.

.....

A Mother's Love

There at birth
Grinning at
My beginning
Your wide eyes
Looking me over
From head to foot
Soon snuggling
Into your breasts
Suckling
The nectar of life
Taking care of my needs
Little did you know

You were planting seeds
Afternoon naps ended
With candies under my pillow
To soon
Did school start
I hated us to be apart
Single mother of four
You went to work
Those special times we had
I treasure
Like an old miser
I secretly take those memories
And bask in them
Then hide them away
Obligations got in the way
Of mother & son bonding
I grew up quick and hit the road
Many lonely nights
I laid beneath stars
Wondering how you are
From bunkhouses in BC
Freight trains up north
Married 25 years
Two darling daughters
A Down Syndrome son
I've been blessed
Thanks to you mother
Seeds of love
Planted long ago
Continue to grow...

.....

Mother's Shoe Box

I remember as a boy
Watching my mother
Once a month, in the evening

Sit alone in the kitchen
With a shoe box full of bills
Deciding where each hard earned dollar
Would go
Single working mom
Four kids, 1 year apart
A nurse on the graveyard shift
Maternity ward, Winnipeg General
I used to wonder how would I pay
Those bills when I was older
Mom did her best
Five of us in a two bedroom apartment
Three boys to a room
Mom in one,
A pink curtain down the middle of the dining room
Made a bedroom for sister Joyce
Mom cried softly some nights
For the loss of our father, her husband
Gone to Holland at sixteen (WW11)
A soldier in the Korean War
Never returning the same
Soon disappearing forever
Lost in haunting nightmares
That plagued his young soul
We were casualties of war
Mom did her best
With little help
From family or community
Somehow we made it
Through lean times
Mean times, hungry times
Trapped in the double work day bind
I thank you mother
For sacrifices made each day
To ensure, a family, we could stay.

.....

Our Log Home

Love at first sight
Our soon to be home
Golden logs tightly fit
Looking over Stuart Lake
On an acre lot
Tina and I agreed
It was worth a shot
All that we sought
Post & beam, open ceiling
Uniformed logs in every room
Antique wood stove
The heart of our home
Tina, the light of my life.

A Scottish Highland lad
From the North-end of Winnipeg
Carried his Maori bride
Over the threshold
Of their Canadian home
Warm in winter
Cool in summer
Always filled with love.

We grew our first garden
Assisted by daughter Rhiannon
Soon baby Tessa arrived
Our German Shepherd: Kumi
And tom cat: Socrateeth
The logs could grow no more
Yet...there was life
Between the walls
Of our log home.

.....

You Were There For Me

: Tina, my soul mate of 25 years.

You were always there for me
You made living fun
You were my exit
From the highway of life
I never looked back
We had a family
You showed me what love was
You were the reason
I chose the open road long ago
Destiny awaited us
You from Aotearoa
I, the North-end of Winnipeg
During winter days, as a boy
I thought of Polynesia
My great grandfather came to Canada
On a ship called Polynesia
Married a woman named Martina Thompson
You, Tina Thompson, a Polynesian
It was meant to be
For you and I to meet
Together for an eternity
To have three children
It was written on the Trade Winds of time
Before we were born
Like two Cedars in a forest
Separate at first glance
But our roots intertwined
Beneath sacred ground
You were always there for me
I will be there for you.

.....

Rhiannon

Oldest daughter of ours
What joy you did bring
Into our working class life
Happy and well behaved
You loved watching me shave
Fragile Rock and off to bed
Awoken to you crying
For Dot and the Kangaroo
Heart of gold
Full of compassion
Sweet and innocent
Like your Maori mother

Now you're married
A family of your own
Our grandson fills the void
Of not having you around
Circle is completed
I see the resemblance
In the face of your son
Reminds me of a time
You looked to the stars
And said:
Look Daddy, there's
God's Christmas decorations!

Rhiannon I love you
How I enjoyed watching
Mother and you play
Only six months new
When first I layed eyes
Upon you
I knew then
We were meant to be
Blended together with love
Reconfirmed the day
I walked you down the aisle

It was worth it all
Just to watch you smile
And say to Chris: I do.

.....

Tessa

My darling daughter brightens
Everyday. I was there at birth
As you entered Earth. Here to protect
Not frighten. Your presence did enlighten
You're the reason for my existence
Divine plan brought us together
I'll be there matters not the cosmic weather
You're gentle as a feather, sweet as candy
Kind as mother, wise beyond your years
I will wipe your tears, scare your fears
Tessa, I love you as a father was meant too
There is no greater love, I'm sure.
I've taught you the way of the world
Now you're a woman with a pure heart
You're of the light, be prepared for the fight
God chose you for a reason, fit for any season
Each day on this planet I do not take for granted
My days numbered, I take strength in knowing
One day you will be a mother
Delivering children of your own
Your smiling face and comical way cause me
To chuckle in the middle of the day
My struggles and aspirations were paid in full
When God delivered you to me
Darling daughter you're so precious
I love you more then diamonds and gold
During times I strained with life's heavy load
You gave me strength to continue
From birthday cakes, furry pets, and perfumes
You were never a bother

I'm proud to be your father
My love for you can never be known
There are no words to describe the amount
It's higher then the North Star
Deeper then a mermaids ocean
Heavier then a mountain of silver
My Highland heart beats proud
When I see you standing tall
I pray you never fall.

.....

Cat Buy Me Love

Where have you been my feline friend
As she jumps thru our bathroom window
Out for the night, now I'm back
So, what of it?
She meows around the children
Gaining their support, allies
Then to the couch to relax
I watch this camouflaged cat
Breathe and twitch while sleeping
Dreaming of terrorizing mice and birds
The magical cat starts to bring me
Into her trance
Believing how special she is to us
And how old she is getting
Until the can opener is heard
The feline awakes and dashes to the kitchen
Like a new born kitten
Kids call her Precious
I refer to her as Deadbeat
Here by a request from my daughter Tessa
I was there when she chose you
At the SPCA nine years ago
In a cage with ten whining kittens
I found a blue eyed Siamese

And a cool Persian
No, Tessa chose you
Climbing to the top of the cage
Crying and looking so pitiful
A plain Jane, homely butt, kitty
Destined to become a homely butt cat
Now, Tessa has moved over seas
And left you with us...oh joy!
She raised you like a mother cat
You even came when she whistled
We all miss her now
Especially you and me
When I lay on the couch for a nap
You jump on my lap
Both dreaming of Tessa
And her love for us.

.....

Brandon

Our special boy, sent to us from High
On loan to give us joy
Messenger of hope to help us cope
Humble philosopher who will not stumble.

He came late one night...oh what a fright!
Three hours in this world, soon on a flight
He beat the odds, surely sent from the Gods
A Devine plan brought our Down Syndrome son
To join his clan.

Knows not anger, hate, or discriminates
A product of love, gentle as a dove
He's very silent and proves to be reliant
Lives for today, always ready to play.

Our dear Brandon was chosen at random

Only ten and can not hold a pen
Imparts to me what is right
Even though he can't write
Others do not have this insight

Product of light, not here to fight
Sacred trust, I assure you, worth the fuss
A ready grin, void of sin
Angel in waiting not capable of hating

Special needs child, gentle as a lamb
In need of compassion, love, and support
The Creator gave us these traits
To guard their innocense and fate.

God put souls on Earth to protect:
Sparrows fallen from nests,
Lost puppies and stray cats,
In a way, Brandon is like that
To watch without reason
Gone in any season.

A philosopher prince of love
Let my gentle son be a reminder:
Children are so precious
Sleep well Brandon, you'll not be abandoned.

.....

Still Thinking of Lloyd

Stopped into Tabor Foods
To get some ice
As I have for seventeen years
Margaret
Good will embassador
Of the neighbourhood
Always has a cheery: "hello"

Knows everyone by name
Ringing me thru, she said:
Today is the 17th anniversary
Of Lloyd's death
We had 27 wonderful years together.
I'll always be thankful for that.
I could tell by the look in her eyes
That she loved him so.
A real sincere love
Not counterfeit
The one society's been missing
I was given a glimpse
Of the real thing
The way love was meant to be
For two people
Thank you for that Margaret
I know Lloyd is patiently waiting
For his love of 44 years
One day holding hands again:
Him in his red serge
You in a floral summer dress
As you did when long ago
Your love for each other
Did merge...and will forever more.

.....

Enchanted Summer Course

Summer course at UNBC
Five intensive days
Enter Dr. Transken
Looking like she should be at an airport
Wheeling in suitcases and bags
Like a medieval gypsy
She spreads her wares
Designed to enlighten us
She plunks & prances round the room

Half speaking, half singing
Arms uplifted
Moving too and fro
Like weird willow/oak/birch branches
Magical star dust falls
From her activated body
I envision:
Fairies and elves
Flying around, urgent weeds, odd flowers
In mystical gardens
Existing in her aura
Gently...oh so gently...
Leading us thru dark forests
Of pain, sorrow, and abuse
This journey is cold, barren
But...yet
One witnessing walk, we, as counsellors
Must explore
We exit that cruel place
Instantly warmed
By heat our class searching-talked
Into existence.
Enlightened & emboldened by:
Cards, readings, poetry,
And more...oh...so much more.
We can now assist others
To shine their light
On the dark horrors of abuse
Thanks, Si, for seeds
pliable useful mud,
star dust left in our hair.

.....

Lavender Woman

:for Jacqueline Baldwin

How she loves to dance
And sing
Growing flowers
Of Lavender
In the Spring
Causing beauty
To abound
For all things
A soothing soul
Does Lavender Woman posses
Sharing her marvel for life
With everyone she meets
Weaving words of comfort
And joy, in a splendid way
Fortunate are they
Who breathe the aroma
Set forth by Lavender Woman
Her fragrance causes others
To dance and sing
Under moonlight dim
In meadows emerald green
Song birds awe in envy
Whenever she sings
Children gather round
Drawn by her love
Lavender Woman
The planet is joyous
Where ever you're found.

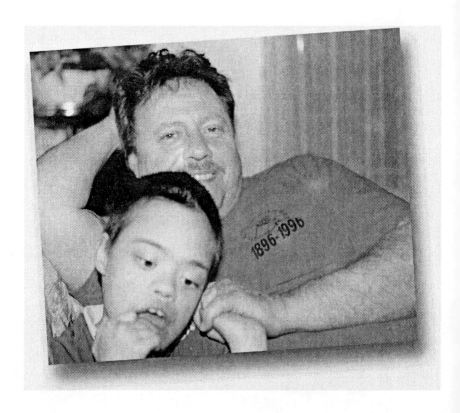

THIS CONCLUDING MOMENT IN THE CONTINUING/
BEGINNING CONTINUING... CIRCLE....

I came to explore the wreck.
The words are purposes.
The words are maps.
I came to see the damage that was done
and the treasures that prevail.
From Adrienne Rich's 'Diving into the Wreck', <u>The</u>
<u>Fact of a Doorframe; Poems Selected and New 1950- 1984.</u>
1984, New York: W. W. Norton and Company.

Theatre is pretending you know what you're doing when you
don't know anything for certain and what you do know
seems to be changing all the time.
Six days out of seven I am a creation, someone who relies
on luck, lust, and determination. Dorothy Allison. 1995.
<u>Two or Three Things I Know for Sure</u>. New York: Penguin
Group. p. 27.

My knowledge is traditional, theirs is academic, my
designation is mentor/elder, theirs is doctor of
philosophy/professor, my leadership are chiefs and grand
chiefs, theirs are mayors, premiers. They are intellectuals,
intelligentsia, I am wise and powerful. They are literati,
sociologists and medical professionals. I am a story teller,
an orator, a healer and a shaman. My research is wisdom,
theirs is science.
I want to re-member, but the membership of what to what
is no longer. The members in my mind are rooted in old
knowledge, ancient schools of thought, oratory and modern
literary history, theatrical being, sociological contexts much
different, much less acknowledged, but no less valuable.
When I remember origins I become whole.... Lee Maracle. "No
Longer on the Periphery." <u>Contemporary Verse 2</u>. Spring
2000. Vol. 22, No. 4. Theme Issue: edge/wise: Canadian
Women's Writing at Century's End. pp. 36-37.

...The girl is bold, smiling in her sleep, as if she knows what people wonder, as if she hears the old men talk, turning the story over.

It comes up different every time, and has no ending, no beginning. They get the middle wrong too. They only know they don't know anything. Said by the character Pauline in Louise Erdrich's, <u>Tracks</u>, 2001 reprint, New York: Perennial, p.31

We are connections from the past to the future. We are the candles lighting darknesses. We are comrades watching each other's backs. We ain't patriarchs or handmaidens to patriarchy's intentions. We are re-writing, re-visioning, we-being. We are re-wording and differently performing some of the scripts of gender/ class/ culture... We are moments and mobilized in creative continuing circles...

    This Ain'ters, 2003

Printed in the United States
15846LVS00004B/1-57